PRAISE
for *The 7-Cent Decision* and Amber Voight

"Amber has been a student of our profession since the day I met her. I am so proud of everything she has accomplished. I believe *The 7-Cent Decision* will help you break through your own excuses and find the right mindset to become a network marketing professional."

— **Eric Worre,** founder of NetworkMarketingPro.com

"Amber radiates fun and confidence, and people are immediately drawn to her. She lays it all out in the *7-Cent Decision*. I love her story and her philosophy for attracting people versus chasing them. Each page draws you in with specific bullet points for building a strong and successful business. Amber is the real deal."

— **Jordan Adler,** bestselling author of *Beach Money* and network marketing professional

"By starting early, Amber appears wise beyond her years. *The 7-Cent Decision* is a simple, straightforward, step-by-step guide to creating success in network marketing. I can't think of a more powerful read to help you succeed in the network marketing profession."

— **Chris Gross,** CEO of Gabriel Media Group, Inc. and cofounder of *Networking Times*

"I remember when Amber reached out on Facebook and we connected. I was really intrigued by her, as she was different. She just *got it*. She was the real deal. She had a unique gift for the network marketing business and was only in her twenties! Since then, I have seen her grow into one of the brightest, most powerful, and most popular stars in the network marketing profession. *The 7-Cent Decision* is one of those rare reads that must become a part of any success library. Brilliant! This is one of the absolute best books ever written for the network marketing profession."

— **Doug Firebaugh,** CEO of PassionFire International

"This book is filled with the most critical components for achieving success in network marketing. Getting started in business is like learning to ride a bike. You can't just read a manual and expect to 'get it.' You learn by experiencing it for yourself. Amber's willingness to be vulnerable, along with her genuine desire to help others, provides invaluable lessons for any reader who wants to mitigate their learning curve.

— **Janine Finney,** coauthor of *The Flip-Flop CEO*

"Amber Voight nails it with *The 7-Cent Decision*! If you want to be a successful network marketer, follow her lead and do what she shares here. Amber gets right to the point and shows you exactly how to make your network marketing business a success."

— **Todd Falcone,** speaker and trainer

"*The 7-Cent Decision* is a smart, practical book that will teach you precisely how to grow a successful network marketing business. Amber has the heart and soul of an entrepreneur and delves deep. She will inspire, motivate, and persuade you that success is possible provided you have the right mindset and a keen interest in learning how to do it *right*."

— **Valerie Bates,** bestselling coauthor (with Mark Yarnell) of *How to Become Filthy Stinking Rich Through Network Marketing Without Alienating Friends and Family*

"The last few years, I have watched Amber Voight from afar, as we are both network marketing professionals. I love her energy, her style, and her willingness to be real! She exemplifies that the only person you need to become is the best version of you. The reason Amber is so successful is that she genuinely cares about people. She has created an amazing business and community because of her passion for network marketing and for life. In *The 7-Cent Decision*, she shares exactly what she does and what she knows will help you create the life you deserve."

— **Kathleen Deggelman,** leading
network marketing professional

"Amber Voight's story is exactly why I love the network marketing profession. I can just picture her at six years old with her briefcase, an entrepreneur at that young age, already wanting to be her own boss! Amber shows us how her huge heart, coupled with unbridled determination, created her success. She is a master at building a team of people she attracted based on who she is and how she shows up in the world. I finished *The 7-Cent Decision* with even more respect and admiration for Dave and Amber Voight, and I will be passing this book along to my team!"

— **Denice Chenault,** leading network
marketing professional and life coach

"We love Amber and Dave Voight! After 25 years of experience building large teams in network marketing, I can say with certainty that *The 7-Cent Decision* is a book everyone in the network marketing profession wants to read. This book will inspire and guide you. For busy people who want to achieve lasting success, *The 7-Cent Decision* is packed with specific, real-world, practical examples of exactly what to do, say, and learn so you can build a large team and grow as a leader. Sylvia and I recommend this valuable book to anyone building a network marketing business."

— **Garrett McGrath,** president of the Association
of Network Marketing Professionals

"Amber shares in a very authentic and heartfelt way the essence of what network marketing and being a servant leader is all about. We have a simple business, and we have a people business. Amber keeps it all about those two concepts. Anyone who wants to duplicate her results will study this book and take action. Even the title, *The 7-Cent Decision*, is brilliant. You'll have to read it to know why!"

—**Jackie Ulmer,** network marketing
professional, author, and trainer

"Amber Voight is an inspiration! *The 7-Cent Decision* is filled with practical tools to help anyone who has heart and drive to achieve tangible success. This book will change the way you see yourself and your power to create an incredible, fulfilling life."

—**Michelle Gielan,** bestselling author
of *Broadcasting Happiness*

"*The 7-Cent Decision* was written by one of the most successful network marketing distributors in our profession today. Amber is one of those rare people who genuinely cares about others without expecting anything in return, and she speaks from the heart. I believe these two unique features are why she has been able to do so well in the business. She created her own massive success, and now she is willing to share it with others through this book."

—**Jim Lupkin,** coauthor of *Network Marketing for Facebook*

"Amber is the kind of person you can't help but love. You'll love her even more as you get to know her story and how she persevered. She is creating quite a ripple effect within the network marketing profession. *The 7-Cent Decision* is so authentic and real, I can't wait to share it with everyone I know. Full of simple and easy-to-follow steps, with stories and quotes that inspire, *The 7-Cent Decision* will be up there with the must-read books in the network marketing profession."

—**Amani Zein,** leading network marketing
professional and coach

The 7-Cent
DECISION

The 7-Cent DECISION

Creating Your Best Future
through Network Marketing

AMBER VOIGHT

with David Voight

NETWORKING Times
MOVING THE HEART OF BUSINESS

Published by Networking Times Press, Chatsworth, CA

Distributed by Networking Times, Chatsworth, CA

For ordering information or special discounts for bulk purchases, please contact:

Networking Times
11418 Kokopeli Place
Chatsworth, CA 91311
818-727-2000
www.networkingtimes.com
www.7centdecision.com

Cover design and composition by Accelerate Media Partners, LLC

Copy editing by The Media Concierge, LLC

ISBN 13: 978-1-934550-10-6

LCCN: 2016901312

Printed in the United States of America

Contents

Foreword . . . . *xiii*

Preface . . . . *xv*

Introduction *1*

1 Get Your Mindset and Attitude Right *9*

2 Balancing Family and Business *19*

3 Know Your *Why* *27*

4 Personal Development and Self-Talk *37*

5 The Law of Association *45*

6 The Art of Non-Recruiting *55*

7 Social Media Tips *67*

8 Starting Your New Distributor Off Right *79*

9 Team Motivation and Creating Duplication *89*

10 More Leadership Tips *99*

11 The Power of Events *109*

12 Belief, Gratitude, and Faith *119*

Acknowledgments *129*

Recommended Resource List *131*

About the Author *133*

The best you can do for anyone is to thrive fully and be willing to explain to anyone who asks how it is that you are thriving, and what it is that you've discovered— and then, just relax and trust that all truly is well.

—Abraham, via Esther Hicks

Foreword

If you ask Amber Voight for the strategy she and her husband Dave used to catapult their two-income family from 7 cents in the bank at the end of the month to a lifestyle most only dream of, she would tell you, "I just love everybody."

My love affair with Amber Voight began long before I had the pleasure of meeting her in person. She burst into my life, as she has for so many, through the power of the internet, her signature pink hair and dazzling smile encouraging and inspiring me through videos and posts every day on YouTube and Facebook.

To a techno-tard like me, Amber was something of a superwoman who quickly became a legend. "How does she do it?" I often wondered as I saw her build a thriving business and massive following on social media. I was thrilled to see her empower so many with her message. Because Amber has such a zest for living, finds such joy in the wonderful world of network marketing (and has so much belief in its power to transform lives), I knew she was destined to change many, many lives over the course of her career.

A little over a year ago, I finally got to meet Amber in person. As I got to know her, I came to realize she is a legend for good reason. She has an inspiring story—the stuff Hollywood makes movies about. She is a multifaceted entrepreneur, housewife, and mom who homeschools her kids. She seems to have found a way to do it all and have it all.

What impressed me the most about Amber was her level of belief. Some people hope, some believe, and others—very few—*become* belief. They have such certainty, there is no room for doubt. She *knows* she can do it, and she knows *you* can do it, and if you spend enough time in Amber's presence, you will know that you can do it, too.

I was thrilled to find out Amber was writing a book because I want everyone to have the opportunity to be in her orbit in some way. I have little doubt that her story will inspire you and her teachings will transform you. The way she breaks down the skills and articulates the mechanics of network marketing will enlighten you and help you move forward on your journey to success.

Most importantly, in the end, you will know that you have a mentor out there who truly cares about you, believes in you, and is cheering you on!

Because Amber just loves everybody . . .

–Lisa Grossmann, multimillionaire entrepreneur

Preface

The 7-Cent Decision

I always wanted to be an entrepreneur. When I found network marketing, I knew this was my chance. I joined my first company when I was 17 and it took me almost 10 years before I met with significant, sustainable success. I have no regrets, and don't wish anything had been different, because it was all part of the journey. My life today is a direct result of everything I learned about mindset, relationships, people, and the network marketing profession. Looking back, I can see how every challenge I faced shaped me into the person I have become.

My entire growth process and journey to success started with one defining moment I remember vividly. It happened in the fall of 2012. My husband Dave and I were both working as hard as we could, and we still could not get ahead. We were stressed out, and our family was struggling financially. One day we checked our bank balance, and after all our bills were paid, we had exactly 7 cents left. That's when we made *the 7-cent decision*, and we knew our lives were about to change forever.

DAVE **Dave Voight**: I realized I had been working my tail off for nearly 10 years at what I thought was a great-paying career, and at the end of the month, all we had left was 7 cents. I was working for a system that was not rewarding me or my family the way I wanted it to. When I saw the 7 cents, I figured, "What do I have to lose?" I was also tired of being mentally beaten up every day at work by people telling me what I could and couldn't do. The 7-cent decision was a shift we both made in our minds. We wanted to change how we were living and build our own future.

Our jobs left us with only 7 cents at the end of the month, so we decided we needed to change paradigms. We didn't have anything to risk, so it wasn't a hard decision. Once the decision was made, it was swim or sink. We always knew and felt we were worth more than 7 cents, more than the wages we were making and the limits our bosses imposed. We decided, "Enough. We are going to make our own wage. We will never have only 7 cents in our account again."

Another thought that led me to the 7-cent decision was realizing I wanted to contribute more. I believe God doesn't plant a desire in your heart without giving you the means to fulfill it. The bible says we were created to give from the overflow. How could we give from the overflow with only 7 cents? We wanted to give more! Today, my biggest dream is to provide value and help as many people as I can to build a network marketing income. This is also my goal for this book. Now that I've told you a little about *The 7-Cent Decision*, let's go back and take a look at where Dave and I came from.

Amber's Story

I was born in 1985 in North Minneapolis to teenage parents. I always knew my mom and dad loved me, but being kids themselves, they weren't ready for responsibilities that come with parenting. Inexperienced and lacking resources, they didn't always make the best decisions and learned by trial and error.

Growing up, I spent a lot of time at my grandmother's house. I was very independent and started taking care of myself at an early age. I prepared my own food, did my own laundry, and even registered myself for school. Being able to do things other kids normally don't do made me confident and resourceful—two character traits that would help me greatly later in life.

My entrepreneurial journey started when I was six years old. All I wanted for my birthday was a briefcase. I always had a big personality, and I knew I wanted to be a business owner. When my parents finally gave me my first briefcase, I joined a direct sales company for kids. I found out about it on the back of my *Highlights* magazine. The company had a fundraiser that allowed kids to earn cash and prizes.

I called and ordered all the supplies to get started. As soon as the materials arrived at my house, I put on my Sunday dress, loaded my briefcase with all my catalogs, and went door to door offering my products. When my mom found out what I was doing, she almost had a heart attack. We didn't live in a safe neighborhood, so she instantly put a stop to it. That was my first direct sales venture, at six years old.

In eighth grade, I dropped out of school and started working odd jobs. Seeing my parents struggle inspired me to take charge of my own life. My upbringing has made me the person I am today, and in a funny way I'm grateful for the challenges my family went through when I was young, as it made me strong and has helped me on my journey to success.

The hardest thing about my childhood was the instability. My parents had unstable jobs. They had an unstable life, so we would always move. By fourth grade, I had attended 10 schools. The best thing about my upbringing, however, was that I was surrounded by people who loved me. Although they often made poor choices, I came out strong, whole, and complete because I always felt loved.

DAVE Amber and I have been together since we were 17. My childhood was definitely different from hers. I grew up in a stable home. We always had food on the table and clothes to wear. We never missed any necessities. We lived in a trailer park, and I didn't think anything of it. It never dawned on me that my parents didn't make a lot of money, because we had everything we needed. I was pretty carefree as a kid.

Growing up I started hanging out with some kids who didn't have the best influence on me. We did things we shouldn't have been doing. We'd drink and party and smoke weed. I would get involved in petty theft—stupid stuff like that. I was totally the opposite of Amber, who never got into trouble and was a stay-at-home girl—and that's actually how we met.

I went to a party with a few friends of mine at some girl's house. Amber knew this girl because she lived down the road from her. This girl's dad kicked us out in the middle of the night, and Amber lovingly took us all into her house and said we could spend the night. Amber was babysitting her younger sisters while her mom was out at a New Year's party. I feel God really placed us together that day.

We fell in love, a year later we got pregnant, and we got married. We were both working minimum wage jobs at the time, mostly restaurant and Walmart jobs. As our family grew, we moved into government housing where you just pay 30 percent of your income for rent. We both had full-time jobs and Amber's mom helped out with the kids. Amber's mom and dad had become dedicated and supportive grandparents.

Thankfully I've never been without a job since age 15 and I kept advancing in my career. By age 20, I was a low-voltage electrician and got a job that allowed us to move out of the low-income housing. We moved into a family home in Buffalo, Minnesota, and we lived there for about three years. That's where we started realizing that even though we both had decent jobs, they wouldn't lead us to where we wanted to go.

➤ Taking Entrepreneurial Baby Steps

Somehow we always knew something bigger and better was in store for us. I had dabbled in network marketing since I was 17 and kept experimenting with different companies. Seeing some of my friends having success, I would join their company. When it wasn't working for me, I would find someone else who had success and join their company. I didn't know anything about personal development or leadership. When I failed, I thought, "It must be the compensation plan; it doesn't pay enough."

Or I would blame the product. "It's too expensive. Nobody wants to pay that much." For several years I jumped from company to company, and when things didn't work out, I blamed everything but myself. Eventually I asked myself, "What's the common factor here?" That's when I realized, *it's me*! That's when I started working on myself and my mindset. The shift also happened thanks to Dave, who kept telling me to open up my mind for success. Once *I* decided to grow and change, that's when things started to happen.

 **DAVE** At one point we decided to stop looking at network marketing and

explore traditional businesses. We opened up two tanning salons, which quickly did well. Then a network marketing company came along that caught our attention because of its car program. We joined that company and it became a launch pad for our success in network marketing. Seeing how traditional businesses work definitely helped us look at network marketing as more of a business than a hobby.

It was actually one of my customers at the tanning salon who got me back into network marketing. She scheduled a tanning appointment, and then canceled and scheduled again. This happened a couple of times. I finally made a house call to her, which is what she wanted all long so she could give me a protein shake from the network marketing company she was involved with. She talked to me about her company and I joined. I went to my first company convention, and that's where the magic happened.

We didn't have the money to attend this event, but I was told that if I wanted to be successful I had to do what successful people do. They were going to be at the event, so I had to be there. I didn't pay my rent that month and went to the convention instead. I sat in the back of the room with my arms crossed thinking, "These people are crazy. Why are they all so happy? What's wrong with them?" Dave kept telling me, "Just open your mind."

Remembering our "7-cent decision," I eventually let go of my judgment and resistance. I went to work on myself and my business, and I fell in love with the network marketing profession.

Today, my deepest desire is to become a generic network marketing trainer who helps thousands of people across companies and industries. By sharing my journey and the lessons I learned, I want to give you the tools and belief to succeed.

Are you ready? Let's get started!

Introduction

Ever since I became successful in network marketing, people have been asking me, "How did you do it?" I love to teach what I have learned and show others exactly what I have done. I wrote this book to help you believe that you too can succeed in network marketing and to give you the tools and strategies to get to work.

People often email or Facebook message me with specific questions about different parts of the business, and I don't have time to answer them all. My goal for this book is to provide answers to pretty much every question I have been asked in my 13 years in the business so far.

The first thing I want you to know is that success comes as a result of cultivating the right mindset. As the saying goes, when we change the way we look at things, the things we look at change. When we got started in this business, Dave and I had to make a mindset change. I was much more skeptical than he was in the beginning, but he kept saying, "Just have an open mind. Just do it and see what happens." We did, and things started happening for us.

I had to stop worrying about looking silly or about friends and family telling us that what we were doing was not going to work, or that we were wasting our time—all those negative comments that come at you when you make a change. Other people's opinions held me back in the beginning.

I was also quite negative myself, sitting with my arms crossed in the back of the room at my first company training instead of participating in "silly" exercises—until I realized the silly one was *me!* I was judgmental about people who had what I wanted and about a system that was obviously working to provide it.

When we started building our business, we didn't have any friends who were financially successful. We didn't have many positive influences around us, so we threw ourselves into the teachings of the late business philosopher, motivational speaker, and author Jim Rohn. We listened to NetworkMarketingPro.com founder and author Eric Worre's trainings. We read books and watched anything we could find on YouTube. We even got rid of our TV for a while to free up time for personal development.

We consciously limited the time we spent with people who did not want to grow or change, and instead we started associating with people we met at events, especially those who were more successful than we were so we could learn from them.

We also got clear on our *why*. Everyone wants to make money, but that's not your *why*. What do you want to do with the money? "I want to have the freedom to stay at home with my kids." Why? "I want to be there for their first steps, share all the precious moments." Dig deep into your why. Once you know your *why*, *what* you do has much more impact.

To create success, we had to change our self-talk. I still catch myself sometimes thinking, can I really be like this or that leader? Can I really do this? I choose to talk back at myself, "Of course I can. Stop talking like that!" We all have that negative voice in our mind, but we can override it with a positive one. "Yes, I can do this. There's no reason I can't. I'm meant to help people succeed!"

Another topic we will cover in this book is the art of non-recruiting and non-selling, because it is the foundation on which I built my entire business. I use a form of *attraction marketing* that boils down to this: I don't think of myself or what's in it for me if somebody joins my team. I don't think of the money that's going to add to my check. My entire focus is, "How can I help this person?"

Believe it or not, I've never *asked* anybody to join my team. I don't say, "You want to sign up? I think you'd be really good at this." Instead, I listen to people. I make lots of friends. I build lots of connections. I'm interested in *them*. We have two ears and one mouth, right? Make sure to always listen twice as much as you talk.

Whether I'm looking through my newsfeed or overhearing conversations in life, I just listen. Often I hear women say, "I've got to run and go to work," or, "I had to miss my son's recital," which gives me an opportunity to plant a seed. Through my own actions, through my own lifestyle, and through how I talk to people, others see the difference between my life and theirs. Eventually they ask themselves, "How can I get this?"

I especially practice this kind of listening on social media. I've signed up 300 people in the last two years, and every single one of them came to me as a result of my social media activity. Instead of posting, "Join my team for $99," I'll post a picture of my kids at the park with the caption, "I still work hard at my network marketing business, but I love that I can create my own view!"

A post like this makes people ponder: "I'm sitting here looking at a cubicle. I wish I could do my work at the park with my kids right now." At some point, some people may decide to approach me and say, "I've seen your amazing posts. I've seen that you're home with your kids. You get to homeschool and still are able to afford vacations and nice things. How can I get this in my life, too?" That's the perfect time for me to introduce them to my business opportunity.

Attraction marketing works especially well on Facebook, as long as you do it with the right mindset and intent. You need to approach others thinking, "It doesn't matter if I benefit or not. How can I serve this person?" When you have this attitude, people feel it in their hearts. They sense that you genuinely care about them, and they're going to want to do business with you.

This attitude requires faith and belief that what you give out always comes back to you. I didn't always have this faith. I developed it over time through personal development and learning about the Law of Attraction. This Law is based on the premise that *like attracts like*. Think positive thoughts? Then positivity will come your way. Think negative? Negative is what you will attract. God created this law for us to use so we could have better lives. My faith and belief came as a result of knowing that I can create my own destiny. I just need to focus on the right thoughts and attach the right feelings to those thoughts.

When Dave and I were struggling financially, all we could think of was, "How are we going to pay our bills?" Guess what? The bills just kept coming in, and we still didn't have any money to pay them. Truly, what you're thinking about is what you attract. You have to choose what you focus on. If you're focusing on the negative, you're going to get more of it.

Even—or *especially*—if your present situation is not ideal, focus on what you'd rather see. One night when we were living in our old trailer home, I went to bed asking myself, "What can I do to get myself out of this situation?" Imagining answers to this question helped me feel better and think more positive thoughts. This activated the Law of Attraction, and sure enough, my life started to improve.

Part of thinking positively is being grateful. For our family, things didn't start to get better until we were grateful for what the universe had already brought to us. Even living in that mobile home with the holes in the wall, we tried to make it look nice. We painted the walls and put rugs on the floor. We tried to make the area we lived in the best we could, and we were grateful for the roof over our heads.

Once we became truly grateful for what we had, a few months later, we moved into a beautiful home we once couldn't have imagined living in. When you are thankful for what the universe has already brought to you, it's going to bring you more. If you're not thankful, you're going to stay stuck where you are—until you start changing your attitude.

In addition to teaching you the right mindset, this book will also show you the practical steps I took to build my network marketing business—how to approach people on Facebook, how to get a new distributor started right, and how to lead a team and create duplication. We'll cover how to deal with team gossip and drama, how to handle excuses and procrastination, and how to create team unity and motivation.

Finally, we'll talk about the power of momentum—how to create it and sustain it on your team and with each new person you enroll. My goal is to get people a check as soon as possible and to really ride the wave of their initial excitement. The faster they start, the easier it is. It's like going up a hill on your bike: if you go slowly, you may fall down. Once you reach a certain speed, it's much easier to keep going. That's how momentum works.

Once you learn how to take the right actions and culti-vate the right mindset, you will start to see some results. But you need to take action consistently for an extended period of time. You can't just work on your mindset and expect success to happen. You have to go out there and create it. Once you start seeing a little bit of success, don't stop. You have to continue to take the actions while nur-turing yourself with personal development resources.

Success in network marketing is a never-ending process. I see people who say, "I hit the top rank. I should be making a ton of money. I can stop doing personal devel-opment," or, "I don't have to keep recruiting. I don't have to keep talking to people." Then they wonder why their checks aren't growing as much as some of their col-leagues' checks are. Realize you will always continue to grow. Don't stop being a student of the profession once you start seeing success.

Your network marketing business is an ongoing journey. It's a fun journey. Make it fun! It can be anything you want. It can be spiritual. It can be enjoyed with family and friends. It can be whatever you want it to be. You create it. You create your own "life of your dreams."

Get Your Mindset
and Attitude Right

*"If you can change your mind,
you can change your life."*

—William James

The way our mind works is a direct result of how we were raised. Most of us were taught, "Get good grades. Go to college. Get a great job." Then retire when you're 65 on less than what you were making, which wasn't enough to live on in the first place! To most people, that's normal.

As entrepreneurs, we're often looked upon as abnormal. "Get a real job!" is what most people feel like telling us— and what you're going to run into with most people you approach about your business. When you join network marketing, you will have to face everybody—your peers, your coworkers, your family. Most likely, they all have that mindset.

I want you to know it's okay to be different. Don't hate them. Don't get mad at them. They just don't know any better. They were raised to believe that "get up, go to work, go to sleep, repeat" is what we're supposed to do until we retire and die. When they see something different, they don't understand, so they judge it as bad or stupid.

When we have this negativity around us, sometimes we can get sucked in. We all have doubts. We have different voices in our heads, and even though we've made new choices, there might be some old, negative voices left. How do we neutralize them and stay positive?

➤ Nurture Your Mind with Personal Development

At times when we encounter negative people or our own doubts, it's up to us to do what we can to lift ourselves up. I always go back to personal development when I'm feeling a little frustrated or when any kind of negative thoughts pop into my head. I nurture myself by plugging in to positive messages, because a negative thought and a positive one can't occupy the same space.

This might mean you pick up a book. You go on Facebook and find quotes from people you respect. Usually I like to hear things, so I either go to Audible.com or YouTube. I may pick up *Think and Grow Rich* by the late Napoleon Hill or listen to an audio program by personal development legend Jim Rohn. These are my main go-tos when I'm feeling a little down or defeated. It's normal to feel this way at times, regardless of what business you're in.

Whether our business is real estate, a salon, a mom-and-pop store, or network marketing—as an entrepreneur, we're all going to get frustrated from time to time. It's part of building a business. It's not a super easy thing to do. If it was, everybody would do it. Thankfully we have YouTube and many other wonderful resources to pump ourselves up so we can keep going and take our business to the next level.

➤ Journal to Help You Stay Focused

Another activity that helps me with my mindset is journaling. I do it on my phone, but you can also write in a paper journal. One thing I started doing just recently (since I learned it from Eric Worre) is at night I write down my goals for the next day. Write down your to-do list, and also write down the way you're feeling that day. Write down what you're grateful for.

Gratitude is a critical component for setting the Law of Attraction in motion. If you want to feel more grateful, start to appreciate what you have. I wasn't able to move out of that mobile home I was living in until I started appreciating it. I tried making it better, painting the walls and decorating, just making it as nice as I could, and I was thankful for it. Until we can appreciate what we have, we're not going to get anything better.

Track Your Activities and Results

Once you incorporate journaling into your business, you will start to feel different. Write down the people you talked to that day, what you said that worked well, and anything you learned. You can use this as a record to go back to when you experience a slow time in your business. When this happens, see what you were doing when everything was going well—who you talked to, what happened during those days—then duplicate and recreate the success you once had.

Let's say you had a week when you totally rocked it, and now you're having a week when not much is happening. You're not selling anything. No one's interested in the business. Now you can go back to that week when you absolutely rocked it, and right there on the page will be exactly what you did that day—who you talked to, what you were feeling, what you were thinking. Next, you can decide, "Maybe I should go back to doing what I did that day. It worked. Maybe I should go back and talk to the girls over at that insurance agency. Maybe I should go to another town and talk to another insurance agency."

Because you were writing things down, now you can learn from the past—what you did and the results you created.

➤ Learn from Your Successes—and Failures

When you journal this way for a couple of weeks, you may be able to see a pattern, and you can create a recipe for what works. "When I was really successful, I did this. I did something similar this week, and I was really successful. But last week I didn't do much. Let me see my to-do list. What did I do that day? Who did I talk to? I didn't talk to as many people as I talked to the week when I was successful. So that may be the problem: *I'm not talking to enough people!*"

Journaling about your journey is kind of like creating a map of success by writing things down. You can go back and review the past, and from there you can program your future. Just as I sometimes learn from watching my own videos, I also can learn from writing things down. You can see the trends of what you're doing right and the results you're having. Make sure to incorporate journaling into your business and into your team culture.

DAVE As I listened to audio programs and read personal development books along with Amber, I started to notice the things I was learning in real life with the people I worked with every day. I noticed people would have a positive or negative outcome based on whether their mindset was positive or negative.

I used to work in the trades, so when we would show up to do a job, we'd be assigned different people to work with. I would notice how some people would show up with a negative mindset and start vocalizing, "This job is going to be terrible. This one's just going to be really hard." Then the work would be hard. When we'd show up with a different crew, some guys would be totally positive and broadcast the mindset, "Yeah, this might be a little tough, but it won't be so bad." As a result, we all had a much better experience. Working with different people, I learned how a different mindset had a totally different outcome on the job we were doing.

Mindset is everything. To have a new life, you have to build it in your mind first. When I lived in our mobile home, I didn't think that was my end. My end was my dream house and my dream car. I had a life already built in my mind—and I held on to that picture in my mind. You can't let your current situation be known as your reality.

Once you have your mindset in order, you have to take action. *The Secret*, a movie based on the Law of Attraction, was amazing, but it was missing one key element: *action*. You can't just be thinking about that ideal picture in your mind all day; you have to be doing things every single day, consistently, that lead you to that picture in your mind. That's how the Law of Attraction works. Activity—the *right* activity—is a good way to neutralize a less-than-positive mindset. Taking action will make you feel different. It will change more than just your mood. Action will change your entire mojo and energy.

➤ Work the Business into Your Life

Women often feel overwhelmed when adding a business to their lives. When this feeling comes up, I say to them, especially when they are new, "This business is meant to fit into your life; don't try to fit your life into your business!"

When we give 100 percent of ourselves to our business at the expense of our family's needs and values, we tend to forget why we're doing it. What overwhelms and burns us out the most is having no time for ourselves. I had to learn to really work the business into my life instead of the other way around. You don't have to work this business 100 percent of the time. You get to choose when you work it and how many hours a day.

Let's say it's two hours a day for now. Be completely focused during those two hours. Just work it 100 percent during the time you're able to give. Perhaps you can have your sister, a friend, a neighbor, or your husband take the kids for a couple of hours. Then fully focus on your business and do the money-making activities. I've seen many people burn themselves out by working on things that aren't producing income such as checking email or making Facebook graphics.

➤ How to Allocate Your Time and Focus

Here is how you should allocate your time and focus: 50 percent of your time should go to creating new relationships with potential customers and team members, 25 percent should be spent on personal development, and the other 25 percent you should be working with your existing customers and team. If you follow this schedule, you won't burn out. Again, you don't have to work your business 100 percent of the time, just 100 percent of the time you're able to give.

To prevent burnout, you have to work it in a way that's sustainable. For instance, you can't give up things that are vital and critical to the health and balance of your family. There are some things you can give up to create that free time to do what you need to do to launch your business. One of the biggest is watching TV. We gave up watching TV completely when we were "going on a run" to reach one of our previous ranks by a certain time. We even got rid of our cable service.

Watching TV can be a big time waster. Give it up. Give up the gossip magazines, the *US Weekly*, the *Star* magazines—all of that stuff. Fill your free time with personal development. Give up the radio in your car and replace it with educational audio programs. These are things you can easily work into your life without changing a whole lot.

Chapter 1
Summary

1. Nurture Your Mind with Personal Development

2. Journal to Help You Stay Focused

3. Track Your Activities and Results

4. Learn from Your Successes— and from Your Failures

5. Work Your Business into Your Life

6. Decide How to Allocate Your Time and Focus

Balancing Family
and Business

> *"The key to keeping your balance*
> *is knowing when you've lost it."*
>
> *—Unknown*

Trying to make time for life, while being completely absorbed in your business, is not sustainable. Instead, take care of yourself and your family first, and fit your business into the nooks and crannies of your life. Soon you'll realize you can incorporate your business into your life. I took my kids for a walk to the park, and as they were playing on the jungle gym, I talked to a few prospects. I was making follow-up calls as I pushed my kids on the swing. Women are great multitaskers. You can do two things at the same time and still feel like you have time freedom as you're working.

➤ A Typical Day—When I Got Started

When I first got started, I worked the business a lot. I was excited. I was still trying to work my life around my business. I hadn't made that shift yet. As my kids' home-school teacher, every morning I would give them their assignment, and then I would start working my business. I spent most of my time, probably 70 percent, meeting new people on social media, mainly through groups, and building relationships.

My approach for getting to know people is not trying to *be interesting*, but *being interested* in what they have to say about their life. Building those friendships and new relationships turned into new customers and team members, and many referrals. (Read more on this in chapter 7: Social Media Tips.)

After a few months of doing this, I still spent half of my time creating new relationships, but by then I started working more with my new business builders and doing team activities, traveling, and training. If you're not in a position where you can travel a lot, don't worry—you can do most of this virtually via Skype, Periscope, webinars, Google Hangouts, and conference calls.

Use Live Video Streaming for Team Meetings and Presentations

Periscope, a video-sharing app, is big now. It's having a major impact on how we do business in network marketing. I use it all the time. The other day I was out kayaking and in the middle of the lake, I did a Periscope Q&A. I had 300 people on, just asking questions, and I would answer them one by one. People love to be able to see you. When you go live, your followers get notified and they can log in.

I actually had a woman who didn't even know what network marketing was. She had been following me online and asked, "What's network marketing?" I was able to answer her through Periscope with everyone else listening in. When we were in Las Vegas at a recent training, entrepreneur and bestselling author Jordan Adler stopped over, and we did a Periscope together—his first one! Now he's obsessed with it. Periscope is a really cool tool for us. It's kind of like a live broadcast.

I also use Periscope for presentations. Let's say we are doing a business opportunity night for our team and everyone invites prospects. I can set up my laptop and present live in several people's living rooms. We can invite attendees from all over the world to log in to that live presentation through Periscope. It's like having your own reality show where viewers can ask questions.

Applying the Law of Averages

During times when I'm pushing hard to reach a new rank in our company's compensation plan, what changes is how many people I talk to in a day or week. Obviously, I'm focused on talking to new people every day, but not as much as when I'm pushing for a new rank. To measure how I'm doing, I record who I talk to, just as Jim Rohn teaches in his audio on the Law of Averages.

Every time you talk to somebody, write down their name, the date, and if they were interested or not. Keep track of every single person you talk to. Soon you're going to see a pattern. For instance, I've talked to 20 people and one said yes. That means if I need four people to join my business by the end of the month, I need to talk to 80.

Keeping records will show you your average, which is going to get better over time. I did this when I was running for a top position in my company. I started with an average of 1 in 50, so I knew if I wanted to sign up two people, I needed to talk to 100 people. I kept going and logging my results, and in three months I raised my average to 1 in 10.

Tracking activity and results can be a big motivator for people. Most newbies in the business don't write anything down. They just kind of go with the flow and work haphazardly. I'm telling you: *write things down*, stay organized, and keep those journals. Jordan Adler shared with me that he has kept every single journal he has written. When he got his helicopter pilot license, he said, "I knew this goal was in my journal somewhere," so he went through all his boxes and dug up a journal from 10 years ago where he said was going to get his pilot's license. Writing it down had helped him reach his goal.

This Business Is All about Sharing Stories

When you go back and look at your old journals, you're going to be amazed at the things you only wished you had, the things you wrote about, and the goals you reached. Same with your Law of Averages log. Save it, because you're going to be able to go back and see how your averages got better and better. From 1 in 50, mine went down to 1 in 30, and now it's 1 in 10. You can share your results with your team. Our job in network marketing is all about telling stories. Each journal becomes a collection of stories.

Also, there's this principle: "What you measure, you can improve." Before you read any further, here are a couple of things I want you—and everyone on your team—to start doing: get a journal and write down what you're thankful for, your goals (with target dates), and your to-do list. Keep a log of everybody you talk to, and keep track of your conversations and conversions. This will allow you to measure your results—and improve them.

Involve Your Family: Make Dream Boards and Learn Together

Dave and I help our kids think like entrepreneurs by telling them things like, "You can be your own boss." When our son says, "I want to work at a pizza place," I say, "You can *own* a pizza place." We teach them they can be and do anything they put their mind to. A lot of parents tell their young kids, "You can be anything you want," but as they get older, the parents say, "You can't do this," or "You can't do that." Most kids hear "no" way more often than they hear "yes." Always empower kids by telling them they are capable. Help them see that the world offers infinite possibilities.

We homeschool our kids, and last year we started a class where we study Jim Rohn together. We had our son listen to YouTube videos and we asked him to write a report on Jim Rohn. Involve your whole family, especially if you have a spouse who has more of a negative mindset, as this may help him or her to come around. When you're doing your personal development, make it a family affair. Grow and dream as a family.

Another thing you can do with small kids is make a dream board together. Ask your kids about their own dreams. Ask, "What do you want?" Even if it's just ice cream, cut out an ice cream cone, and put it on their dream board. Everybody in the family can make one together, or you can each make your own.

Teach Your Kids to Think Like Entrepreneurs

Watch some YouTube videos together. Listen to books or programs on Audible instead of having the radio on in your car. Listen to something that's going to help your kids expand their minds. Incorporate personal development throughout your day so your entire family can grow and learn together.

As we started listening to audio programs in the car, my son complained a little at first. He said, "Jim Rohn is boring. He's just a farmer from Idaho." As our kids started listening more, they liked it more. My two small boys love it now. They know it's going to help them be and do better in school and with their friends. They see mom working in her business, and they want to be in network marketing when they're older, because they see the time freedom.

Your kids may not always accept what you do, and if they don't want to be network marketers, that's fine. You do want to awaken and nurture their entrepreneurial spirit, because it can help them no matter what they do later in life. Even if your kids may be a little resistant at first—after all, Jim Rohn doesn't have the most exciting, upbeat, kid-friendly voice—keep doing it. Be consistent with it. Eventually, they will start to realize, "This is just something we do together," and later in life, that's what they're going to remember: in our family we sat down and learned together.

DAVE It's hard for some husbands or spouses to wrap their heads around not going to a 9-to-5 job to collect a paycheck. I grew up in a household where my dad had an entrepreneurial mindset, so he would always be looking for different ways to make money outside his regular workday. If you are a husband or spouse who does not have that entrepreneur's mindset, let me tell you: it may be a little hard to accept at first, but be willing to open your mind and try something new.

Chapter 2
Summary

1. A Typical Day—When
   I Got Started

2. Use Live Video Streaming for
   Team Meetings and Presentations

3. Apply the Law of Averages

4. This Business Is All About
   Sharing Stories

5. Involve Your Family: Make Dream
   Boards and Learn Together

6. Teach Your Kids to Think
   Like Entrepreneurs

Know Your Why

> *"People don't buy what you do,*
> *they buy why you do it."*
>
> —*Simon Sinek*

Your *why* is what makes you jump out of bed in the morning. What's the reason you keep going? For me, it started out with my kids. I wanted them to have a better life than I had growing up. When we talk to our prospects, we want to ask questions to understand their *whys*. Why do they want to do this business? If they say it's for money, I ask more questions until I get to the real reason. It's never just about the money. Why do they need the money? This is how you get more into the depth of why they want to build a network marketing business.

Someone's *why* could be, "I had a difficult childhood. I want my kids to have a better childhood," or "My husband works so hard; I just want to relieve him of some of that burden." Unless you drill down to that deeper reason of why they want to do the business, they won't have that personal connection to their *why* in their heart. You want to find out why they need the money because that's what will emotionally connect them to their business goals.

Ask Questions to Get to Someone's Deeper *Why*

To go deeper into a person's *why*, I'll ask, "What do you want to do with your business? What are you looking to get out of this business?" If they say, "I want to make more money," I'll say, "Okay, what would you do with that money? Where would it go?" They might say, "It would go to my kids, to help them get their school clothes." Now I get to their real *why*. They want to do it for their kids. I keep asking questions until I get to the core of their *why*.

We all have two ears and one mouth, so we need to listen twice as much as we talk. As a leader, we must ask questions instead of assuming things. Some people are motivated by money; others may have money and don't care as much about that part. What they want is more friends. Perhaps their *why* is that they're lonely and are looking for a sense of community. Others want to be part of a team and exercise their influence and leadership.

Your *why* isn't always everybody's *why*. Especially when you're recruiting, listen and ask open-ended questions like, "Where do you see yourself in this business five years from now?" The answers to these questions are going to reveal people's *whys*.

Different Personalities — What Makes Them Tick?

According to Tom "Big Al"' Schreiter's personality colors, I am a "red" personality, which means I'm dominant, money-motivated, and crave recognition. I may have a "yellow" personality on my team who wants to do network marketing so she can help more people. It might not be about the money for her. If I'm explaining to her how she can earn free trips, make money on the side, or cover a car payment, these things don't matter as much to her. She's thinking, "Who can I help with this?"

Often, leaders assume people are joining the business for the same reasons they did. This may not be correct. You're not going to build a heart-to-heart connection if you only see your point of view, if you can't see someone else's perspective. Learning about the different personality types can be very helpful here.

Learn to Dream Again — and Dream Big!

Many people are not even in touch with their *whys*. Because they have money struggles, they don't allow themselves to dream. This reminds me of a question I learned from legendary speaker and author, Bob Proctor. It was the title of his audio, *What Would You Change If Your Annual Income Suddenly Became Your Monthly Income?* Use this question with your prospects and follow up with, "Would that make a difference in your life?" I've only had a resounding "yes!" in answer to this question.

You may think it's a stretch, but that's actually what happened to Dave and me. In just a couple of years, our yearly income became our monthly income. Ask bold questions! "What would you do if money were not an object?" or, "If you had all the money in the world, how would you spend your days?"

If you ask just one question, "Why do you want to do this business?" the answer may be, "Because I want free product." This isn't a strong enough motivation to build a business— and is probably not the true reason. Keep drilling down with your questions and keep listening. As leaders, we don't listen enough. We listen to respond, not to understand. We also need to be listening to the cues. People give us their answers in ways they may not even know. We have to learn to pick up on that. We have two ears and one mouth for a reason.

➤ Be a Friend Who Offers to Help

When you interview your prospects, you don't want to sound like a businessperson going through a list of 20 questions. Don't be a drill sergeant or an investigator, but ask them as a friend. Feel into your heart and connect with your own genuine desire to help: "As your business sponsor, I want the very best for you, so let's talk. Tell me a little bit about yourself, about your family, about your life right now, and where you see your life in five years. Let's dream big. Let's open up our minds." Then just listen.

Imagine you're having a heart-to-heart conversation with a friend. As you are listening, make sure to jot down some notes. You will want to remember some special and personal things about your team members. When I'm talking to new people and they tell me things like their kids' names and ages, I'll write that down so I can remember them for future conversations. When they're feeling defeated, I can remind them of their *why*.

DAVE Your *why* may change over time. When you start, it might be to get your kids some school clothes. After you achieve that, look for your next reason *why* you'd want to achieve the next milestone. Your why changes over time, and that's all right. It's actually what needs to happen for you to grow into the leader you want to be.

➤ Write Down Your *Why*—and Your Team Members' *Whys*

For the Law of Attraction to work optimally, we can't just keep our *whys* in our heads. We have to get it down on paper. This is part of my process when I talk to new people who join my team. I have them write down their *why*, and I also have them make visual reminders. For one of my girls, her *why* is her children. There isn't a lot of extra money, so she can't take her kids to do fun things like an outing to the movie theater. Her backdrop on her computer is now a picture of her kids having fun. We did that on purpose so that every time she looks up, that vision gets imprinted in her mind.

If your why is to retire your husband, write it down. "I want to retire my husband in three years," and add a date. Once we set a date, it sets things in motion. Often we say, "We're going to do this," but until we actually schedule it, it doesn't happen. I always have new people write their goals with dates. (See more on that in chapter 8: Starting Your New Distributor Off Right.)

Activate the Law of Attraction with Visual Reminders

When I notice someone's a little frustrated, or they're not really engaged in their business, I say, "Let's remember your *why*. I want you to take that notebook out and reread it." Writing it down is critical, as is having visual reminders throughout your home, on your phone, or in your car. When I was working to get to the first leadership rank in my company, I had reminders everywhere. I need to make some new ones, but right now I do it on my phone: I have our next rank, which is my goal, visible each time I look at my phone. At this point, my *why* is simply to help as many people as I can to be successful.

We also regularly update our vision board and place it where we see it all the time, like in our kitchen. Dave and I dream together and decide what our next goal is going to be. Then we'll put a visual reminder on the mirror in our bathroom. In our old house, I wrote on the bathroom mirror, "I am going to be a National Director." Every time I went to brush my teeth or wash my hands, I would see it. Keeping your goals and dreams top of mind is critically important.

We make sure to share our vision with our kids, either by making dream boards or by talking about them. When we reach a goal, we go out for dinner or to a movie. We let them know how our vision came about and celebrate together—and we express gratitude.

Center through Meditation; Connect through Celebration

There's one more *why* Dave and I share. Ever since we were 17 years old, we've wanted to start an organization to help educate young parents. We were young parents, and we had no resources. Our family didn't know anything about finances or credit. For instance, I was encouraged to get the most expensive car I could afford when I was 18. I know many young parents who are in similar situations. They don't know how to create a resume or how to look for housing. We want to teach them some of the things we learned.

Last but not least, each night before we go to sleep, we reconnect with the part of our vision that brings us the most joy. Then we read or listen to something that's going to open our hearts and minds. We meditate and pray together. We sometimes use a meditation app from self-care expert Andrew Johnson. Eric Worre shared it with us when I was at his house. It's a guided meditation program with a visualization component, and it's targeted toward our profession. For instance, you can program it to help you envision what it feels like to reach that next position. It's a wonderful tool you can use any time, but the best time is right before you go to sleep. We lie down, close our eyes, and focus on our breath. We follow the suggestions for full body and mind relaxation.

It's okay if your mind wanders during the meditation. Even if you fall asleep, your subconscious mind is still hearing the suggestions. If you are new to meditation, you may get distracted and think, "I can't do this." That's not the case. You're listening on another level, even if your mind's somewhere else. You're still getting the benefits. Meditation is a powerful tool to help you focus, so make sure to incorporate it into your life.

Chapter 3
Summary

1. Ask Questions to Get to Someone's Deeper *Why*

2. Understand Different Personalities— What Makes Them Tick?

3. Learn to Dream Again— and Dream Big!

4. Be a Friend Who Offers to Help

5. Write Down Your *Why*—and Your Team Members' *Whys*

6. Activate the Law of Attraction with Visual Reminders

7. Center through Meditation; Connect through Celebration

Personal Development
and Self-Talk

*"Work harder on yourself than
you do on your job or business."*

—*Jim Rohn*

S ometimes our self-talk is, "I can't do anything different than what my parents did," or, "I failed at this, I
failed at that, I'll probably fail at network marketing,
too." Remind yourself to rise above your past. You can

break that pattern. We build our own walls of limitations, and my goal is to help you bring your walls down.

When I started my business, I had a voice in the back of my head saying, "This isn't going to work. You've tried this before." Every time a little thought like that popped into my mind, I would plug myself back into personal development. I would go watch a Jim Rohn video or crack open a personal development book. I would redirect those negative thoughts into learning and knowing that I'm growing myself to get better.

➤ Bring Down Your Walls of Self-Imposed Limitations

I also tell my team to watch out for negative self-talk. Whenever you're having those negative thoughts, you need to reach for your personal development resources. Personal development is going to help you get out of that slump, and it's going to pump you up again, because you can't hold a negative and a positive thought in your mind at the same time.

When I'm having negative self-talk, as soon as I notice it (my body getting all tense and my breathing shallow) I stop what I'm doing, pick up a book, open up my Kindle, or fire up my Audible—and I'll start reading or listening to something inspiring or uplifting, because it changes my mindset right away.

➤ Plug in to Personal Development Programs

Another approach is to ask yourself specific questions to shift your thinking and expand your vision. I learned this technique from a training I attended a while ago. Here are four steps you can take to neutralize negative thoughts and emotions, and some questions you can ask.

1. **Test your reality.** *What's my evidence for and against my thinking? Am I jumping to negative conclusions? How can I find out if my thoughts are actually true?*

2. **Look for alternative explanations.** *Are there any other ways I could look at this situation? What else could this mean? If I were being 100 percent positive, how would I perceive this situation?*

3. **Put it into perspective.** *What is the best thing that could happen? Is there anything good about this situation? Will this matter five years from now?*

4. **Use directed thinking.** *Is this a way of thinking that will help me achieve my goals? What can I do that will help me solve this problem? Is there something I can learn from this situation to help me do it better next time?*

Asking these questions will totally change the way you talk to yourself. It's not easy and it takes time, but with practice, you will be able to make a switch in your thinking.

Over time, you will be able to tell when a negative thought comes into your mind, and you will learn not to let it take over. You will be able to redirect it to something positive or ask yourself some questions to see if this really is a big deal.

➤ Raise Your Awareness about Your Thinking

When we ask ourselves, "Will this matter in five years?" the answer most often is, "No, it won't." Then we can see perhaps we are being a little hard on ourselves, or we are blowing things out of proportion, or we are being overly dramatic or emotional. Once we set our intent to catch each negative thought, we raise our awareness about our thinking. You will see that with practice, it gets easier and easier.

We recently took our little boys to see the movie, *Tomorrowland*. There is a mention of a "good wolf" and a "bad wolf" in your head. When they are fighting, which wolf wins? It's the wolf you feed. What a wonderful message—and not only for kids! It really comes down to, *"What thoughts am I feeding?"* If you are feeding the negative ones, you're going to get more negative results. It all goes back to the Law of Attraction.

> *"Be mindful of your self-talk. It is a conversation with the universe."*
> —David James Lees

The first step is to notice when your thoughts are turning against you or your mindset is going downhill. In most situations, it happens gradually. The question is, how do you quickly realize what's going on so you can interrupt the pattern? In other words, you have to be aware of what happens before you can shift directions. I've learned that any time I talk to myself and I'm not feeling very good, it's time to make a conscious shift from self-defeating thoughts to self-empowering ones.

Let's say you have low self-esteem. Instead of thinking, "I'm not capable," or, "I don't deserve this," you can switch your thinking to, "I'm learning to be confident," or, "Every day I feel more worthy of my success." If we continually shift our self-talk to what we want to see and have, we will create exactly that. For instance, I'm really bad at spelling, so I tell myself, "I'm becoming great at spelling." It helps me. I practice and tell myself I'm getting better, even though I'm not good at it *yet*.

➤ Replace Self-Defeating Thoughts with Self-Empowering Ones

I used to practice Tae Kwon Do, and when we had to break that board, the instructor said, "You have to think about it in your head over and over. See yourself breaking that board. Hear yourself breaking that board." When you do that over and over, and you go to break that board, it breaks. When you're talking to yourself in your mind about a certain situation, you need to imagine and focus on what it would feel like to be in that situation. For breaking that board, what will your foot feel like when it goes through the wood? Your mind doesn't know reality from fiction. If you focus on how things will happen, they seem to happen exactly that way.

DAVE I agree 100 percent. Whatever you want to have happen, play it out in your head over and over. This creates a pathway in your brain. Then once the situation comes to you in real life, you're ready for it because you spent countless hours preparing for it. Everything exists first in the mind. Everything that's created on the outside was first someone's thought, plan, or dream. That's how reality gets created. A quote I firmly believe in is by author Peter McWilliams: "Our thoughts are so powerful we can't afford the luxury of a single negative thought."

This is especially true in network marketing. This business is not easy, so you can't afford letting your thoughts go downhill and negative. It takes a while to develop that routine. It's okay if a negative thought pops into your mind and you can't catch it right away. It takes practice. Don't give up. Don't say, "This must not be for me." Keep going because—just as with any other skill—it takes time to develop. Being able to sort through your thoughts and monitor them and direct them is a skill you can learn to master.

➤ Positive Thoughts Are More Powerful Than Negative Ones

The beauty is, a positive thought has a higher vibration, which makes it more powerful. If you have had a lot of negative thoughts about something, and then you switch to a positive thought, it's going to be easier to neutralize the effect of the negative thoughts, because the higher the energy, the more power. In the movie *The Secret*, Rev. Michael Beckwith said, "A positive thought is hundreds of times more powerful than a negative one." I have received plenty of evidence of this in my own life and can promise you will too.

Chapter 4
Summary

1. Bring Down Your Walls of
   Self-Imposed Limitations

2. Plug in to Personal
   Development Programs

3. Ask Yourself Questions to
   Redirect Your Thinking

4. Raise Your Awareness
   about Your Thoughts

5. Replace Self-Defeating Thoughts
   with Self-Empowering Ones

6. Remember That Positive
   Thoughts Are More Powerful
   Than Negative Ones

The Law of Association

> *"Surround yourself with only people
> who are going to lift you higher."*
>
> —*Oprah Winfrey*

The Law of Association was so important in my family's success that I want to dedicate an entire chapter to it. When we were down at our lowest point financially, we were hanging out with people who didn't want to grow or improve their lifestyles. This made it very difficult for us to get better, even after making the "7-cent decision" and realizing that we had to work on ourselves if we wanted our lives to change.

Once we discovered the Law of Association, we looked at those relationships and asked, "Are they helping us, or are they doing the opposite and sabotaging us?" The answer led us to realize we needed to replace some of our friendships with new relationships. We started to seek out the company of people who wanted success, and who wanted to get better—people who were growing. It really helped us turn our lives around. It's a common truth that we become like those we surround ourselves with. The company you keep is what you're going to amount to.

Choose Carefully Who You Allow in Your Close Circles

I'm not telling you to ditch all your friends who may not be successful. Just evaluate who you spend most of your time with. If you're not having success, look at the people you hang out with every single day, and consider their situations. Maybe they have something to do with why you're not having success. If you're doing what they're doing, and they're not having success, then you are not on the path that will lead you to where you want to go.

When I first started my business, I was broke, and so were all my friends. To create success, I had to make up new surroundings for myself. I created a new circle of friends. At first, they didn't know who I was. I chose to hang out with Eric Worre by immersing myself in his videos. I had some upline leaders I chose to spend time with. They were top income earners in my company and in network marketing. I followed them on Facebook. I listened to their trainings and observed everything they were doing. I listened to my new friends—through their videos, trainings, and social media posts—for the majority of my time.

➤ Spend Time with People Who Have What You Want

To my surprise, shortly after I started to hang out with these people virtually, these people who had no idea who I was become my real friends. It's kind of funny how that works. Now I have so many successful friends in my company and even in other companies. I sometimes have to pinch myself! Building these new friendships has become one of the richest and most enjoyable parts of my life. When I have a challenge in my business, all I need to do is reach out to my new friends and they are there to lend me their advice, insights, or support. Of course, they also chime in and cheer me on to celebrate my wins and successes.

I know the same will happen for you once you decide to apply the Law of Association and start surrounding yourself with those people you want to emulate. Jim Rohn famously said we become the average of the five people we spend the most time with. Choose wisely!

DAVE Hanging out with our "new and improved" circle of friends was a little uncomfortable at first. I remember when we were still living in our trailer, we'd listen to Eric Worre's

NetworkMarketingPro.com trainings, and it was quite a contrast with how we were living. He was talking about the motivational speakers and trainers he was listening to in his car when he started his business. Over time, he ended up becoming friends with these people he'd never imagined being friends with. It's funny how the same thing happened to us.

If you're in a tough situation, choose to surround yourself with the people you want to be like, who inspire you, and who are motivating a lot of other people. Identify leaders who have what you want, then do what they do so you can achieve what they have achieved—and perhaps even go a little further.

What If You Feel Responsible to Help People in Need?

I've been there. I used to be the archetypal helper who wanted to save people. I used to be the person who wanted others to be successful more than they wanted it for themselves. Even when they weren't doing anything, I would say, "I see such potential in you!" I used to get so frustrated when they weren't seeing it in themselves. Then I realized everyone is on their own journey. I can't make them do anything. I can't change their situations, even though I know they have everything in them to be successful. Unless they truly want it and do it, it's not going to happen, no matter how much I try to be the hero.

You can't want it more for somebody else than they want it for themselves. You can't save anybody; people can only save themselves. You can give them the tools and the resources, but they have to apply themselves. Don't try to be a superhero, saving everybody. It's not up to you, and it's not your responsibility. All you have to do is walk the walk, lead the way, and if they decide to follow you, great. If they don't, don't fret it. They may come around in their own time—not yours. In the meantime, focus your attention on others who are ready.

The beauty is that successful people usually remember where they came from, and when they see you being a student of the profession, dedicated to growing yourself and growing your team, they recognize themselves in you. They are eager to help you, because now that they have reached some of their own goals, their joy comes from making a contribution and guiding others through that change. Leaders are usually more than eager to help and to welcome you into their circle once they see you're hungry, committed, and coachable.

Work with Those Who Are Working

So who do you spend time with on your team? How do you know who to focus your energy on? When we see people who are making an effort and taking steps—showing up at events, listening to personal development programs, and bringing people to business opportunity calls—we know that's who we need to support. We can't save everybody, so we need to give our energy to those who are showing us by their actions that they are committed. It's a hard decision sometimes. We have team members who don't show up at the local meeting even though it's only 10 minutes away from their house. They're not participating in the webinars. They're not getting on the conference calls. If they aren't doing anything, there is not much we can do for them.

Workshops and generic training events are another place where you connect with this new circle of people and friends. I remember being so excited to meet network marketing leaders like Lisa Grossmann, Jordan Adler, or Garrett and Sylvia McGrath. Today I get messages from leaders I look up to because they want to connect with me. Sometimes I wonder, "How did this happen? What did I do?" It's all about what happens in your mind and what you focus on. Everything starts in your mind first. If you develop the mindset for success, you will start attracting people who are successful. The Law of Association—and its cousin, the Law of Attraction—really work!

DAVE I notice the Law of Association is working even when I'm walking down the street or in the store or at the airport. Usually I was the guy on the construction site, so the guys in the suits weren't talking to me at all. Now here I am, I'm just walking down the street, and the guys in the suits are striking up conversations with me. It's totally different today from what was happening just a few years ago. It's crazy. The vibrations go out, and they just come right back. Like attracts like!

How to Handle an Unsupportive Spouse or Family Member

Sometimes we can't change our inner circle, especially when it's our husband or wife who is the negative influence. Team members have come to me and said, "I'm trying to surround myself with positive people, but the most negative person in my life is my husband. What do I do?" Here's the advice I give them. I say, "Keep working on yourself, and maybe as he sees your growth, and as you change for the better, he'll want to change, too. As you work on your personal development, invite him to listen in or read along with you. If he's still negative, just don't talk to him about your business."

If they continue to be negative after you've invited them to listen and participate, just let them be "your dear husband" or "your dear wife." As you succeed and grow, they're going to notice and want to grow, too. I've seen this so many times in my team members whose spouses were totally against network marketing. Once the wife starts to have little bits of success, the husband often says, "Okay, this thing's actually working." One of these "negative husbands" in our group actually became a speaker at our training events. He now shares the story of his transformation from negative spouse to support partner and advocate of the network marketing profession.

Grow Together, Not Apart

No one can be negative when you show them a check. We have many stories of negative spouses who became positive about their spouse's network marketing business once they saw their partner succeed. In most cases, if the relationship is healthy and meant to be, that's what will happen. We've also seen some relationships come to an end when one person grows and the other person doesn't, or when spouses grow apart. That's just a part of life we cannot control. Thankfully, for the majority of the couples, the personal development they go through as part of becoming network marketing leaders greatly benefits their marriage and family relationships.

Chapter 5
Summary

1. Choose Carefully Who You Allow in Your Close Circles

2. Spend Time with People Who Have What You Want

3. What if You Feel Responsible to Help People in Need?

4. Work with Those Who Are Working

5. How to Handle an Unsupportive Spouse or Family Member

6. Grow Together, Not Apart

The Art of
Non-Recruiting

> *"Everyone likes to buy, but
> no one wants to be sold."*
>
> —*Unknown*

I have to admit when we first got started, I knew nothing about the art of non-recruiting." Don't we all want to recruit people into our businesses? Yes and no. Looking back at some of my old messages from 2012 or 2013, I feel a little embarrassed. I would just randomly message people and say, "I have a huge opportunity for you. You can be one of the three top people on my team. I'm looking for three bright individuals. Here's a link." I'd never even said hello to them. When someone talks to me like this today, I consider it almost spamming.

I doubt a lot of people go on Facebook because they want to be recruited into a business opportunity. Most of us use social media to connect with friends and like-minded people or to be inspired by uplifting pictures and messages. This is exactly what I keep in mind with my social media presence and activities today. My primary intent is to build relationships with my existing contacts and new people. How do you get people's attention and distinguish yourself from all the other "friends" who are trying to connect with them?

Be Interested Rather Than Trying to Be Interesting

One thing I focus on is being interested in others instead of trying to get others to be interested in me. If they're moms, I find out about their kids. I ask what they like to do for fun. I just love on people by giving them my time and talking to them about their joys and challenges. I build personal relationships and really get to know people. Then, once in a while, I say something about my business. Most often I'll post a before-and-after photo or a selfie. If anyone asks what I do, I may share a little more, but I still don't try to sell or recruit them.

I might take a picture of my kids playing at the park and post something like, "I love that I get to create my own view while I'm working." Notice I'm not saying, "Join my team." People are seeing my post and it leaves an impression. They start thinking, "Hmm, I want that. I'm looking at the back of someone's head in a cubicle. I wish I could be at the park with my kids." Another day they may see me at a party having fun with my business partners. We now have a relationship that's starting to build, and they keep seeing things they like and want. Eventually they reach out to me and ask me what I do.

Apply the Power and Ease of Attraction Marketing

This approach has been working amazingly well for selling my product. In fact, I don't have to try to sell it. I just share it and let people make a decision for themselves. It makes my job easy and fun—and something anyone can do! No need to be a salesperson. It's like when you see a movie and you go and tell your friends, "That was a really good movie." You don't have to add, "You should go see it!" *Less is more.*

As I'm building each relationship, I'm also listening. This is key! You're not building a relationship just to chit chat or have fun on Facebook. You have a business mind in the back of your head. In the meantime, you want to be there for people, even if they don't order or sign up. Some of my best referrals have come from people I built relationships with and who aren't customers of mine. They might say, "I don't really wear mascara, but I'm going to send you my friend who does." One of my biggest teams came from this kind of referral. Don't write people off if they're not interested. Still keep building that relationship; just don't spend lots of time on it. If you see them pop up in your Facebook newsfeed, "like" or comment on their posts. It keeps your name fresh in their mind.

Say Less and Listen More — with a Purpose

Back to the listening aspect: when I have conversations with people, I listen with a purpose. I might be talking to a mom who's telling me about her kids, and she says she's bummed out about having to miss a dance recital because she has to work nights and weekends, and her daughter's dance recital is on Saturday. I'm listening for things like that because I might have a solution to offer. I don't really look at it as trying to recruit people; I'm looking more for a chance to share an opportunity with them. If they want it, great. If they don't, that's fine. I'm just going to offer it as a gift.

Now, there are certain aspects of selling and recruiting I want you to learn about eventually, such as how to invite, how to present, how to overcome objections, and how to close a sale. I teach all these skills to my team. As a businessperson, you want to understand more than just one way of selling. However, I practice mainly "attraction marketing" because it works for me. In the beginning, it didn't work as well, because I didn't have any influence. I didn't have anyone who looked up to me. It gets easier as you start seeing some success in your business.

"If I sent you a quick business overview, would you listen to it?"

When someone's interested in my business, I highly recommend the "If I _____, would you _____?" method. For instance, a person messages me, "I would like to hear more about your business." I'll respond with, "If I sent you a quick business overview, would you listen to it?" Then I remain quiet. I don't say another word. Sometimes we overtalk, especially when we're new to the business. We give too much information right away, and it overwhelms the listener. Just ask this one question, and let the other person say "yes" or "no."

Usually she answers "yes," and then I say, "When would you be able to listen to it?" When she gives me a time, I say, "Great, I'll follow up with you after that." Then I send her the business overview in the form of a sizzle call I have recorded on SoundCloud.com. You could use anything from a video, to a call, a recorded opportunity webinar—whatever your upline or company has available. You could even record your own 5- to 10-minute sizzle call. SoundCloud works really well for my team and me. It's inexpensive and super simple. Your prospects call in and hear a few key points about the business—with a lot of excitement sprinkled in.

Then I make sure to follow up. That's where a lot of people fall short. They're scared to follow up. Why did you give them the link if you're not going to follow up with them? They're expecting it! When I follow up, I simply say, "Did you have a chance to listen to that link I gave you?" Then I'm quiet again. I let them say yes or no. If they say no,

I say, "That's fine. I know life is super busy. I have three kids. When would you get a chance?" I keep setting up another follow-up time until they actually listen to it.

Lead the Conversation in a Positive Direction

Most of the time people will listen to the presentation right away because they're excited. After they've listened, I say, "What did you like best?" I ask a question that's going to bring out a positive answer. "What did you find most interesting?" You want to make sure they're not going in a negative direction. You don't want them to start the conversation with, "I don't like that you have to pay $99 to join." You can't come back from a negative right away, so you want to lead the conversation. I do this by asking questions that have only positive answers. If you say, "What did you like best?" they might say something like, "I really like that there's no monthly autoship," or whatever it might be.

Then you say, "I really like that too. I'm in love with this company. I think it could be a nice fit for you. Are you ready to get started?" Then I'm quiet again. I don't over talk. Again, many network marketers tend to "puke up" words all over people. That used to be me—until I realized it doesn't work. Now I say the least amount possible and I let the tools work for me.

Let the Tools Work for You

You can use a tool like *Networking Times*. I taught my team how to use my *Networking Times* Master Networker story (an 8-page magazine article) as a prospecting piece. This kind of third-party validation is powerful! It does the talking for me. It works a lot better than me trying to explain it all. My sizzle call is another tool my team and I use. It's a presentation I recorded in my own voice, and it works well for everyone.

Tools always work. If my company or upline had a good business presentation, I might use theirs, depending on whether it fits my style. If your company doesn't have a business overview that you like, create one. Know that when you're building a network marketing business, you are building your own team and marketing approach. The company's only responsibility is to pay commissions on time and make sure the products are delivered as promised. As a leader, you are responsible for creating your own team culture. You can come up with your own marketing tools, as long as they are within the company guidelines.

➤ Handle Objections with Personal Stories

Here is how I teach my team to overcome objections. Let's say someone wants to sign up, but they don't have the money. Don't say something like, "You're 40 years old, and you don't have $99 to spend? You need this more than anybody!" Trust me, this doesn't work. Instead, empathize and respond with a personal story. Say, "I totally understand. Finding extra cash can be hard. I actually had no money when I first started, and I realized I really needed to make a change. What I did is I looked for things I wasn't using that had a little bit of value, and I sold them. I found an old Coach purse and sold it on Facebook on one of those garage sale groups to come up with the money. Do you think if we brainstorm together and figure out a way, we could make it work?"

Giving a personal story shows that you can relate to how the other person is feeling. When you ask them if they are willing to brainstorm and try to make it work, their answer will show you if the objection is simply an excuse, or if it's a real obstacle they want to overcome. Offering to help find a solution allows you to weed out those who are ready to get started from those who are not.

Another common objection is, "I don't have time." A mom might say, "I have little kids at home. We have sports. I'm not sure where I would find the time." Here we do the exact same thing: relate to people's situation by sharing a personal story. It works with anything. With the time objection I would say, "I totally understand that. I home-school my three little boys. It is crazy around here. What I've found is that you can build this business around your life. I set my kids up with their school work, and then I put my computer right next to them, and we work together. If we brainstormed and figured out a way to make this work for you, would you be willing to give it a try?"

I also add that people who are really busy do the best in our business, because they are always out and about. They are already active and talk to lots of people. That's actually better.

By relating to people with your own personal story, you never make it directly about them. That way you don't risk offending them or giving them bad advice, like "You're too busy? Why don't you quit your job!" You never want to offend anyone or advise them on their situation. We want people to come up their own solutions. If you told someone, "You could quit your job and do this from home and be with your kids," and then the person doesn't take action in her business, she could come back and say, "You told me to quit my job!" *Whoops.*

➤ Use Three-Way Calls for Closing

When it's time to ask for the sale or "close" someone, I always recommend the three-way call. Especially if you are kind of new to sponsoring, get your upline on the phone, and let them close the sale or the recruit for you. It makes it so much easier, especially with a family member or friend.

DAVE Often, your close friends and family (your "warm market") don't see you as the expert. If you have friends you went to high school with, and ten years later you're doing well in your business, they still see you as the high school student who didn't take school very seriously and goofed around. Even if ten years later you're doing better than the person who was working hard on their homework and getting straight A's, they still see you as the goofball and can't imagine you as a successful businessperson. Same thing for those you used to work with: they still see you as their coworker, not as a business owner. In both of these cases, a three-way call can make all the difference.

Three-way calls also use that third-party validation we mentioned before. Here is how it works: When you call your upline in for a three-way call, first edify them. Let's say Dave is on my team, and his cousin wants to join his business. Dave says, "I have my upline Amber on the phone. She is an absolute rock star in our company. She has reached the top rank. She's doing great, and I'm super excited she was able to take a few minutes and talk to us." Then he goes quiet. He can actually mute his phone.

Then I take over and say, "Thanks, Dave, for that wonderful introduction. I'm so blessed to have you on my team." Now I edify him so his cousin sees that I, the big top earner, firmly believe in Dave and am working with him. Then I simply ask the new person, "What have you heard so far about our company?" After he answers my question, I ask, "Tell me a little bit about yourself." We talk a little so I can hear what his current situation is and what his goals are. Then I say, "Sounds like this could be a really good fit for you. Are you ready to get started?" Then I remain quiet and let him say yes or no.

Most of the time prospects are going to say yes. That's how I got into my previous company. My sponsor got me on the phone with his upline, and he used the "Are you ready to get started?" approach. I said *"yes"* even though I didn't know what I was saying yes to! I didn't build that company, but I'm super glad I joined, because I made lots of great friends and connections.

The art of non-recruiting is all about building rapport. You do it with a purpose. You keep your mind focused on getting to know each person and seeing how you can fill their needs or alleviate their pain. If you can help to solve someone's problem, people will want to do business with you.

Chapter 6
Summary

1. Be Interested Rather Than Trying to Be Interesting

2. Apply the Power and Ease of Attraction Marketing

3. Say Less and Listen More — with a Purpose

4. "If I sent you a quick business overview, would you listen to it?"

5. Lead the Conversation in a Positive Direction

6. Let the Tools Work for You

7. Handle Objections with Personal Stories

8. Use Three-Way Calls for Closing

Social Media Tips

> "Marketing is no longer
> about the stuff you make, but
> about the stories you tell."
>
> – Seth Godin

Social media allows us to have easy access to more people than ever before. This makes building a network marketing business easier than it's ever been. Social media is really big in terms of its reach, so make sure you are always presenting yourself the best way you can. One thing I keep telling my team is when you post something *it's there forever*. Even if you post something in the heat of the moment, and then you go back and delete it right away, the damage is done. You never know who might have taken a screenshot or who has seen your post.

➤ Be Cautious About What You Post on Social Media

Facebook visitors form an idea of you from the first time they see your profile. Statistics show that if people don't like your cover photo (the big photo at the top of your page), they're less likely to look at the rest of your profile. Make sure you have a good cover photo with a positive message. People are attracted to positivity, so pick something that looks or feels good. Websites like Canva.com allow you to create excellent graphics. You can even throw your own picture in there and add a quote. You can also do a Google search for "Facebook cover photos."

Next, people are going to look at your profile picture (this picture appears as a thumbnail in all your comments/posts). You want your contacts to create a relationship with *you*, not your children, so don't put up a picture of your kids. I love kids, but this is *your* profile, so show a good picture of yourself. It doesn't have to be professional photography. It can be shot from your smartphone, as long as it's clear and crisp, and you're smiling. Show yourself in a professional manner. Don't portray yourself being goofy or doing anything inappropriate.

➤ Always Show Your Smiling Face ☺

Building your social media presence doesn't happen overnight. It takes time to build up your friends list and develop those relationships. There is a magic number I've discovered. Once you have 2,000 friends, that's when you start seeing a lot more response and engagement. A lot of people come to me saying, "I'm not getting anywhere on social media. The first thing I ask them is, "How many friends do you have?" I typically hear a number between 500 and 800. Then I say, "I have good news and bad news. The good news is: *it's not you*; it's your lack of audience. You just don't have enough friends—which isn't really bad news, because we can improve it!"

Similarly, YouTube starts airing commercials as soon as videos reach 2,000 views—it's just a magic number in social media marketing. A long time ago, when I took a Facebook class and first heard this information, I thought, "I'm never going to get to 2,000 friends." I just want you to know it's much easier than it sounds. Don't be scared of that big number. It can happen pretty fast, especially if you're focused on a few proven strategies to build your friends list.

Join Groups to Make New Friends

A great way to find friends is to join some groups around your interests. For instance, I have an Irish Setter dog. I could go on Facebook and find some Irish Setter groups. This way I am connecting with people I have at least one common interest with, and now we're going to apply our art of non-recruiting. We're not going to join these groups to find recruits. We're going to meet people, get to know them, and make more friends. Again, focus more on being interested in them than on trying to be interesting your-self. That's how I build new friendships.

An important piece of advice: always "hide" your friends list. Someone (a spammer) might try to "friend" all your friends. To find out how to hide your friends list, do a Google search for "how to hide friends on Facebook."

➤ Videos and Photos are BIG!

Videos are big! They are the most popular and widely shared posts. People will watch a two- or three-minute video more quickly than they will read a 30-second text post. Most of us are scared to make videos. My biggest tip: *make the video and post it.* Don't watch it, because if you watch it, you're going to say, "I don't look good in this one. I should have said this better." You're going to pick on yourself and you're not going to post it. We are our own worst critics. Just post it. Even if you're scared to make videos, do it anyway. The more videos you shoot, the more comfortable you're going to get.

Photos are the next most popular posts. To make your photos stand out, add some graphics. Again, Canva.com is a good resource. WordSwag is a great app. You can upload your picture, fade it out or use filters, and you can put a quote over it. It looks really professional. Another DIY design site is A Beautiful Mess—ABM is the abbreviation. These are the three biggest graphic companies I use, and they work amazingly well. I even know graphic designers who use these, so they're really good.

As we've discussed, when posting on Facebook, don't say, "Join my team. Looking for three more people, message me if you want to get in!" Instead, practice the art of non-recruiting and post lifestyle pictures with a positive caption.

If I'm up at the cabin with my husband, I'll post a picture and say, "It's Monday and I'm up at the cabin. I'm so happy I get to work from home." Take a picture of your kids playing outside. When I did this, I signed up probably six people as a result. The caption said, "I am so grateful I'm able to drop everything and take my family on a spur-of-the-moment trip." Moms with jobs are thinking, "Man, I want to be able to do that! But I'm stuck working all weekend." My lifestyle post makes them realize they want what I have, so they reach out to me.

Sometimes it takes several impressions for somebody seeing something they like before they actually contact you. If you post something and you don't get a response right away, don't worry. You have to be consistent. Sometimes it takes a few hits before someone realizes, "I've been seeing this over and over, I need to take action and contact this person." I also post inspirational quotes and any kind of good news. Always remember, people are repelled by negativity and attracted to positive energy.

Positivity Attracts; Negativity Repels

Often people I don't even know, who aren't even on my friends list, message me and say, "I go to your page because you post such positive messages. I have no positivity in my life. Thank you for what you do." These are wonderful messages to get, and I wish everybody would be getting them. We should always be positive on social media.

Even if your day isn't going well, even if you're having challenges, you can still have a positive attitude. Life isn't always rainbows and sunshine. Sometimes we have bad days; that's just being human. Call a friend, call your mom, but don't publicize it on social media. You always need to be positive to attract people to you.

Some might say, "I'm just being real." You can be real, but you don't have to share every negative thought or feeling publicly. Instead, you can turn a "negative" experience into a positive with a change of attitude or perspective.

For example, I once had an upline who had a flat tire on his way to a meeting. He posted a picture of himself dressed in a suit trying to change his tire. The caption said, "Who knew I could change a tire in a suit so well?" He turned a negative situation into a positive instead of ranting about it on Facebook. You can do the same with any negative stuff you come across. It doesn't mean you can't talk about it. You can, as long as you are able to look at it in a positive way.

Apply the 3 Cs—Crazy, Compliment, Confident

When people are liking your posts, they begin to get engaged. Once you have established that relationship, you can try to talk to people on a more personal level. Start liking their posts that come up in your feed. At some point, you could send them a message. Let's say your new friend is a woman who takes a ton of selfies. If you sell personal care products or are in a company like mine, you could say something like this:

"You know, this is super crazy, but you take the best selfies. You would be really good at what I do. Have you ever thought about it?"

Just leave it at that. Don't say anything else. Don't mention your company. We call this the three Cs—*crazy, compliment, confident.* Saying "this is super crazy," kind of takes away the awkwardness of the cold-market approach. Giving them a compliment, "you take the best selfies," disarms people. Then saying "you'd be really good at what I do" boosts their confidence. End with, "Have you ever thought of this?" and don't go any further. This is a simple and effective way to approach people. Always put that compliment in there. People can't get mad at you if you compliment them.

Be Personable and Be Consistent

That's how I work my social media. I make it really personable. Another big key is to be consistent. There are many different social media sites—the main ones are Facebook, Instagram, Pinterest, Periscope, and Twitter. If you're going to be using one for your business, be consistent. For example, I'm not very consistent on Instagram. I'm mostly on Facebook and Periscope, and I'm consistent with these two social media platforms. Every day I post something. But on Instagram, sometimes I go a week without posting anything, and that's why I don't get any business from it.

Whatever social media platform you're using, make sure you post regularly; otherwise, people aren't going to follow you. In fact, if your consistency drops, they're likely going to *unfollow* you, especially on sites like Instagram. Consistency is key, just as Jeff Olson writes about in his book, *The Slight Edge*. Success comes from taking small daily actions repeated over a period of time.

DAVE Positivity is a must on social media. You definitely don't want to air out your dirty laundry on Facebook. It doesn't help your business. It only hurts you. That's just as true for spouses and support partners as it is for business builders. When working a business online, you want to keep a professional image as a couple. Never say anything negative about your partner, even if he or she did or said something that annoyed you. Don't say they're working their business too hard or anything like that. Always keep it 100 percent positive.

Nowadays with social media your team isn't just local. For me, most of my team is *not* local. Just a few years ago, 90 percent of my team would have been within my state. Now 90 percent of my team is outside my state. Having a strong social media presence is especially important if you're building out of state and internationally. I have a fast-growing team in the UK, and when I sign up a new person, we use Skype to go over the starter kit. It's as if we were sitting across from each other in the same room. After that first Skype session, we stay in touch via Facebook.

➤ Use Groups for Building Team Culture

Also for building team culture, Facebook is where everything happens. We have our team group and our corpo-
rate top leader group on Facebook. It's so easy, especially
since most of us are spending the majority of our social
media time on Facebook. I always have my team groups
"closed" so that people can freely share things and not be
worried about non-members seeing their posts.

When creating your group, make it either *secret* or *closed*.
Closed groups can be seen by the public, while secret
groups can't. My group is actually secret, so nobody can
find it unless a member sends them a link and invites them
in. If you create a closed group, its name, its members,
and its description are visible—only the posts in the group
are private to the group.

A Facebook group gives you lots of options. You can set it
up so you have to approve incoming posts before they go
live. I don't do that, because it takes a lot of time. I just
kind of monitor it, and so do my leaders. You can create
a powerful team culture all from hanging out together in
an online group.

Social media also works wonders for training and duplication, because it allows your team to copy what you do. I've
noticed some leaders get upset about this, but I actually
encourage people to copy what works. Let's say I make a
post about one of our products and it gets a lot of engagement, and somebody on my team copies it and posts it
on their wall. If I'm having success with that post, I *want*

them to post it too, because if they have success, obviously that comes around to me.

As leaders, we want to foster duplication. We need to realize if people are copying what we're doing, it means we're doing something right. We *want* people to duplicate what we do. Never get mad if someone copies and shares your ideas. I always tell my team, "If you see me post something you like, feel free to share it." Let your team duplicate you, because it's going to mean more money in your pocket. It reminds me of Harry S Truman's quote, "It is amazing what you can accomplish when you do not care who gets the credit." So true. In leadership, *your ego is not your amigo!*

Chapter 7
Summary

1. Be Cautious about What You Post on Social Media

2. Always Show Your Smiling Face ☺

3. Join Groups to Make New Friends

4. Videos and Photos are BIG!

5. Positivity Attracts; Negativity Repels

6. Apply the 3 Cs—Crazy, Compliment, Confident

7. Be Personable and Be Consistent

8. Use Groups for Building Team Culture

Starting Your New
Distributor Off Right

> "The secret of getting ahead is getting
> started. The secret of getting started is
> breaking your complex overwhelming
> tasks into small manageable tasks,
> and then starting on the first one."
>
> —Mark Twain

I always tell my team that even though we do a lot of our
marketing and sponsoring online, we still need to get
on the phone. Network marketing is a people-to-people
business. This is especially important with new recruits.

When signing up a new person, make sure to call her or him within 48 hours. Welcome new team members, let them know you're there for them, and let them hear your voice. Connecting this way and hearing each other's voice is much more powerful than just typing a message.

Call New Team Members within 48 Hours

A few of my leaders and I did an experiment with this, and we found out that if you wait more than 48 hours, the new person tends to lose some of their excitement. They might run into a negative friend or a naysayer who tells them "these things don't work." So don't wait; try to call the new person right away—as soon as they sign up. Simply say, "Welcome to the team! Here's our training page. I'm going to add you to our Facebook group. If you have any questions, this is my number. Feel free to call me." Forty-eight hours is a critical number if you want to catch the person at the height of their excitement.

Teach People How to Hit Their First Goal

The next thing I do with new team members is I introduce them to our training program. We show them how to hit their first goal, which is to sell $500 worth of product, sponsor three people, and help these three people do the same. If those three people do the exact same thing each month over the next four months, they can hit one of our top positions, which is purple and corresponds to $40,000 in volume. Of course, we tell them this rarely happens, so we shoot for our first leadership level, which is $10,000 in volume. If they do

$500 of sales and add three distributors who do the same in 30 days, then they're going to hit that position.

➤ Send Out a Worksheet to Track Activities

I also send them a monthly worksheet and ask them to write down the names and some details of everybody they talk to. This will allow them to track everything they do. Let's say they have a really great month of July. Come August, their results drop. Now they can go back to July and see how many people they talked to and what exactly they did that month. Thanks to that tracking process, they can duplicate whatever they did during a really good month. We also have a little gratitude section where I suggest they write down what they're grateful for that month, as they are going along. Everybody on my team prints out this worksheet each month and fills it out.

➤ Add New Team Members to Your Facebook Group

After I call my new person on the phone and introduce them to the training, I show him or her how to access our Facebook group. I love our group, because no matter where I am, no matter what time of the day or night, there's somebody there to help. If it's 2:00 in the morning here and I'm sleeping, in the UK, team members are online who can answer a question. I let the new person know we have a huge support group and encourage him or her to make friends and find partners. As I mentioned before, our Facebook group is "secret," which means it's completely private to the people who have been invited in.

➤ Encourage New People to Order Five of Your Staple Products

I also have new people order five of our company's staple products. In my current company, it's mascara. In my previous company, it would be the weight loss shake. Whatever your flagship product is, suggest every new person order five. This is going to do a few things. First, it's going to teach them how to place an order online and how to open up a party if there's a party plan. Second, it's going to teach them how to use the company website. Third, it allows them to have some product on hand for friends and family who might want to try the product right away. Fourth, it's going to get them qualified for commissions. In most companies, buying five staple products in one month will get you qualified.

I do say, "This purchase is optional," because I don't want someone to join my business after they saved up for the starter kit and now think they can't be successful because they can't afford to buy five products. I recommend it, but I tell them, "You can still be successful even if you don't buy any inventory." An added benefit to being able to buy some product is that now they have in the back of their mind, "I bought the kit, I have five of these key products… I need to pay this off before my credit card bill comes due. I need to find some customers for my business." It creates a sense of urgency to get started sooner than later.

Tell New Team Members to Create Their 100-Names List

Now it is time to help new team members create their contact list, as every network marketing company encourages you to make. My target is to get them started with 100 names. People might say, "I don't know 100 people. How do I find these?" My answer is, "You know more people than you think. Your phone didn't come preinstalled with telephone numbers, did it? Go through your contacts and write down the names. Then go to Facebook and Instagram and write down the top people who show up as your friends. There's your list!"

We're not trying to have a huge list. Don't impress me with an 800-names list; show me the people you can actually reach out to. Our goal is to get a name on the list and off the list as soon as possible, so we can put a new name in that spot. We never want to run out of people. Think on and off as soon as possible, and keep adding people and building relationships.

Have Your Team Members Reach Out to People to Build Relationships

Once they have their lists, I want new team members to start warming up those connections. We don't want the first communication to be about their business. If you haven't talked to someone in 10 years, you don't call them and say, "I found this new product and started a business. Do you want to check it out?" We first want to build rapport and make people feel we care about them. I think one key to my success is that I genuinely care about people—and they feel it when they're talking to me. They don't feel like I'm just trying to get them on my team or they're just another number on my customer list.

We want to make that first connection to kind of touch base with people, to get to know them or catch up with them. Then we want to make a second connection. For the third contact, I show my new team members how to use the three Cs—crazy, compliment, confidence—because that's what works well in my business. I recommend they use the 3 Cs for a third connection, which can be made by phone or in a text message.

➤ Offer to Do Three-Way Calls with Friends and Family

In the meantime, I invite the new person to get me on the phone with as many of their contacts as possible. I open up my schedule and ask each new person to introduce me to their friends. "Do you have anybody who's interested? Anybody who you think would be great at this? I'll be happy to hop on a call and tell them about our company or product." I explain to each new person the power of third-party validation and how it takes a while for your friends and family to start seeing you as an expert.

DAVE As we've mentioned before, friends and family are going to see you as they've always seen you. If you used to change oil for a living, they're going to see you as some-body who changes oil, even if you are a top network mar-keter now. They see you as they've always seen you, because they have that memory of you from before you had success. They will take your upline or sponsor more seriously and see them as the experts. Use that power of third-party vali-dation by inviting them to join you on three-way calls.

Use Videos for Ongoing Training and Duplication

Training videos are big, especially for getting new teams started. I created my own *New Presenter Orientation* by simply recording a screen share: I went through my back office and showed people around. "Here's how you order. Here's where you find your sales. Here's where we get paid." I made a whole orientation in video format, which works great for duplication. Anyone can use it, whether they are on my first level or several levels down below me.

Another benefit of video is that it allows people to get to know you more intimately. Let's say you are a network marketing rock star, and you sponsor 100 people a month. It's going to be hard to connect one on one with every single person. After you get someone on the phone for that first call within the first 48 hours, then videos work really well. Instead of talking to those 100 people you signed up, just do a video once a day or once a week, whatever feels comfortable. Eric Worre does *daily* videos. When I finally met him, I felt I already knew him from his videos. Videos are a big help to start people off on the right foot.

One more thing I do is I introduce people to Taxbot. It's an app you put on your phone to track business expenses such as mileage, meals, supplies, and so on. The goal is to document every business expense so you can deduct it from your taxes. This can be very helpful in the beginning when people invest money into their business and don't see an immediate return. When a new person runs into a negative neighbor who says, "Those things never make money," she can pull up her Taxbot and say, "I've already earned government subsidies. So far I've saved $79.81 on my taxes." That's a powerful incentive, so I make this part of my getting-started training as well.

➤ Recommend Taxbot, *Networking Times*, and Your Favorite Personal Development Books

Recently I did a big "getting your team started off right" training at our company convention, and we talked about reading *Networking Times* magazine to build belief in yourself and the network marketing profession. My "Getting Started" worksheet now includes a link to order *Networking Times*, because it really helps with building the right mindset, especially for someone brand new. The magazine has short articles you can read in 5 to 10 minutes, which is great for people who aren't used to reading books.

Most of my new team members have never even heard of personal development. I share with them how my business didn't start thriving until I started growing myself. My signature quote is inspired by William James: "Change your mind; change your life." Personal development is so important you want your new person to get started on something right away. The #1 book I recommend is *How to Win Friends and Influence People* by Dale Carnegie. Even if your team members only read to the second chapter—because they aren't used to reading books—it will start to open their minds for success.

➤ "Getting Started" Checklist

- ☐ Call new team members within 48 hours to welcome them.

- ☐ Teach new team members how to hit their first leadership level.

- ☐ Send a worksheet to track their activities.

- ☐ Add new team members to your Facebook group.

- ☐ Encourage each new member to order five of your staple products.

- ☐ Tell new members to create their 100-names contact list.

- ☐ Have your team members reach out to people to build relationships.

- ☐ Offer to do three-way calls with friends and family.

- ☐ Use videos for ongoing training and duplication.

- ☐ Recommend Taxbot, *Networking Times*, and personal development books.

Chapter 8
Summary

1. Call New Team Members Right Away

2. Teach People Goal Setting

3. Provide an Activities Worksheet

4. Add New People to Your Facebook Group

5. Encourage New People to Order Products

6. Help New Members Create a List

7. Teach Team Members to Build Relationships

8. Do Three-Way Calls with Friends and Family

9. Use Videos for Training and Duplication

10. Recommend Resources and Books

Team Motivation and Creating Duplication

> *"Snowflakes are one of nature's most fragile things, but just look at what they can do when they stick together."*
>
> —Vesta Kelly

As a leader your job is to inspire people. When doing so, always be humble. There's a difference between a humble leader who's inspiring, and a leader who's full of himself and bragging. Always remember:

your success in network marketing is a result of what your team does. To inspire people you need to work your business and lead the way, while giving others the tools to do the same.

Tools can be videos. It can be your knowledge. It is whatever you share with your team members to help them succeed. However, motivation really has to come from *them*. You can't motivate others; we can only motivate ourselves. I often see team members who could do so well, and I *want* them to do well so badly, but if they don't want it for themselves, there's not much I can do.

People are motivated by their own *why*, and as a leader you can help them discover and stay in touch with that *why*. Apart from giving them the tools they need, you can sit down and have a heart-to-heart conversation. We talked about getting a hold of somebody within 48 hours of joining. After you've gone over the practical things, it's time to go over that person's *why* together.

➤ Dive Deep into Their Why

When it's time to have this conversation with new team members, I ask them to write down their deeper why. They can't just put, "I want to make money," because what is money? Money's just paper or plastic. Why do you need the money? Then we delve deeper into it. Maybe they don't want their kids to ever have to worry about where dinner's going to come from. Now you're getting to the real emotional part of why they want to succeed, and that creates motivation.

When your team members are kind of slacking a little, or commenting, "This is so hard," you can remind them, "Remember when we sat down and did your why?" For me, my why is my family. I wanted to get us out of the situation we were in. Somebody told me once, "*If you can look your family in the eyes and tell them they're not worth it, then you can quit.*" I'm never going to be able to do that. That's the power of knowing your *why*.

Another part of motivation comes from creating team unity. There is strength in numbers. That's why we get our team together in Facebook groups and at events, so they can empower and inspire each other. I really love our team groups and the energy they create. Always make sure it's a drama-free, selling-free zone where people come to collaborate and lift each other up. Whenever I see posts that aren't serving that purpose, I delete them and talk to the people who made them.

Create Team Unity with Webinars and Training Calls

One of the best ways to create team unity as a leader is to hold webinars and do training calls. That's going to keep your team active and excited. Some people are self-starters, like myself, but others need that ongoing sense of community to thrive. They need others to hold them accountable. Offering those calls and webinars everyone can plug into every single week is going to help keep their fire lit.

Make sure to include others when leading these calls. Don't be the only person talking, or people will get bored. Let your rising stars who are full of excitement speak and present. This will bring more people to your call, because these budding leaders will promote the training to their entire team and want everyone to listen in. It's also more fun to have different presenters—even people who aren't top earners yet. My team responded well when I started giving the microphone to the winners of our Fast Track bonus. I asked them to explain how they did it. This gave all the brand new people hope, because they felt the speakers were just like them.

In addition to the weekly calls and online get-togethers, we hold live events every 90 days. We all need these events to recharge our batteries. When I first joined, my company didn't have any events outside of our yearly convention. I started organizing quarterly events within my own group. I told my leaders, "We're going to do regional events and trainings. Make sure to bring your teams." Your events don't have to be huge to start; they're going to grow. Having events where you can get recharged and have that face-to-face time is a must.

Organize a Contest or a Friendly Competition

Another team-building and income-producing activity—I learned this from my leader in a previous company—is to have a friendly competition or contest. You can post in your group, "The first to recruit four people by Tuesday wins $50." It's something easy most people can do. Someone will say, "I got one!" Suzy might have two, and somebody else might get three. Then somebody gets five, and that person wins. Look at how many people you added to the team just by creating a little bit of competition! Network marketing teams thrive on this kind of friendly competition.

Recognition is another great way to motivate your team. As the saying goes, *"Grown men die for it; babies cry for it."* Recognition is huge. People often ask me, "What are some of the best incentives you can give people?" I've noticed, in my team, recognition tops all of them—and it's free. I've spent big money on huge incentives like an all-expenses-paid round-trip to our national convention, and then I've done little things like a simple shout-out on a call or a card sent in the mail. I get the best results from the simple recognition. *Bottom line*: you don't have to spend a lot of money right away to start recognizing people. All it takes is a "Great job!" with a quick picture posted on Facebook, or a card in the mail. That's going to be effective and motivate people to keep going.

➤ Use Videos to Create Duplication

This also sets the stage for upcoming leaders who see your videos to want to make videos themselves. Your leaders can teach their teams to do the same. Their videos will be duplicated through their organizations as well. Videos create a big snowball effect of "goodness."

Encouraging people to ask for help is another great way to foster duplication. I teach all my top leaders to do three-way calls for their teams until their new leaders are confident themselves. Duplication is all about putting yourself out there for your team. You'll want to develop lots and lots of leaders; otherwise, you're going to get burned out really fast. Our goal is to develop as many leaders as possible. In our business, we don't want followers.

DAVE We noticed a big change in our business once Amber started doing videos, even though she really didn't want to do them in the beginning. Videos take care of duplication much more easily than telling your team what to do. If you make a team video on how to get started in the business step by step, instead of just calling people on the phone, now they can share your video with everyone they're signing up. Once captured in a video, your content doesn't get altered by being passed around from person to person.

➤ Develop Leaders, Not Followers

I've seen a lot of business people trying to get followers. They want to be the only one speaking on stage. I was like that—in the beginning. Then I learned it just burns you out. You want to lead the way, show others how to get there, and then take a step back and let them lead. Let them be the ones on stage. Let them be the ones doing the calls, because it's going to bring more money to your wallet and more time for your family in the long run.

I don't want you to think that as a leader you're going to have to be available 24/7 forever. Don't think, "I'll always have to do these three-way calls." No, you just do that until you develop that leader you brought into the business to the point where she's ready to fly on her own. Let your people lead as soon as they're ready and able, so you can go back to doing the things only you can do, which includes spending time with your family and enjoying the fruits of your work.

A question I hear a lot is, "How do I know who to work with?" The answer is, "You work not necessarily with those who need it, but with those who deserve it." Spend your time with people who are showing up on calls, attending company events, and making an effort to bring in new people. Don't give your time to those who are saying, "I'm going to talk to four people," or "I'm going to do five home parties," and then do nothing. In other words, *match energy with energy*.

➤ Test to See Who Is Ready to Work

Here's a test I give team members who say they really want to make things happen. Before I commit to coaching them personally, I give them an assignment. It can be anything from reading a *Networking Times* article to watching a NetworkMarketingPro.com video. I say to them, "The first thing I want you to do is to read this article (or watch this video) by Monday." If they come back Monday saying, "My kids were acting up," or "I had to take an extra shift at work," or make any kind of excuse, I know they don't truly want it badly enough right now.

You have to want success as badly as you want to breathe. If you have to pick up another shift at work and wake up an hour early, that's what you do. Building a successful business has to be at the very top of your priority list.

The test you give can be anything; you just want to see if the person will actually do it. To know who to work with, I might call my personal recruits and say, "I only have time to work with a few people who really want to hit that position next month. We're going to go all out. We're going to go hard." You can use whatever language you want. You can add, "If you're super busy this month, it might not be a good time to run, but if you want to do it, I want to lock arms with you." If they say yes, then we go forward, and I give them that first test.

➤ Let People Create Success in Their Own Timing

I had a girl on my team who said she really wanted to "do a run," meaning she wanted to reach the next rank in a minimum of time. To help her, I put her and a few girls in a group chat and said, "We're going to work one on one." Next I gave them that initial task as a test and added, "If you don't do it, you're going to be removed from this group, and that's totally fine. If you're busy this month, with kids starting school or whatever it might be, just let me know. I'm still here for you. Maybe next month we can run together and go one on one." One girl said, "If I can't do this, you're going to remove me from the team?" I said, "No, I'll still love you; you just won't be part of this group chat." Make sure to let your team members know you still love them, even if their timing is not yours.

Everyone works at their own rhythm. As a leader, you work with those who are ready and willing to run with you.

DAVE Jim Rohn used a wonderful analogy. He said, "You're just out there planting a seed. When it finally starts to grow, you get all excited that it's poking out of the ground. Then a bird gets it, or for whatever reason it doesn't grow. You need to know the bird's going to take some of your seeds, and that's fine. That's why you plant lots of seeds, and you just need to love them and be there and care for them." The same goes for how you grow a business with human beings. People will build in their own timing. This month may not be right for them, but three months down the road they may really catch the vision. Everybody has their own timeframe. That's why you want to have many people in the pipeline.

Chapter 9
Summary

1. Dive Deep into Their *Why*

2. Create Team Unity with Webinars and Calls

3. Organize a Contest or Friendly Competition

4. Use Videos to Create Duplication

5. Develop Leaders, Not Followers

6. Test to See Who Is Ready to Work

7. Let People Create Success in Their Own Timing

More Leadership Tips

> "A community is like a ship;
> everyone ought to be prepared
> to take the helm."
>
> —Henrik Ibsen

When you work with people, they inevitably come to you with their issues and problems. I have mostly women on my team, so things can get a little emotional. It is like being in high school sometimes! How do we handle this and keep our sanity?

We have a culture in our team where *we don't gossip*. If a leader comes to me complaining about someone on her team, we won't jump on the gossip train. A quote I really like is, *"Gossip dies when it hits a wise person's ears."* It's so true. If somebody comes to you saying so-and-so is doing this or that, don't say, "Really? She shouldn't be doing that. Make sure you're not doing that." This can easily start a gossip snowball.

➤ How to Handle Drama and Gossip

If somebody comes to me with negative news, I say, "I don't know anything about that, but I do know we have an amazing business, and we're going to do some great things." Then I give them some homework. I say, "Here's what I want you to do. I want you to focus on your business, and I want you to watch this," and I give them a training video that's appropriate for the situation.

I continue with, "After you've watched it, I want you to get back to me and let me know what stood out for you the most." I refocus their attention into a positive direction. That's really the best thing you can do when someone comes to you with negativity, "I don't know anything about that, but here's what I do know." Offer something constructive, and give positive reinforcement.

As you lead people, they are going to come to you with "he said/she said" scenarios, trying to get you on their side. We never want to get caught in this. It creates stress and can be a huge time waster. You don't need extra stress in your business. Drama will make your business so much harder, and I've seen people lose their entire teams because the drama and gossip went too far.

Don't Feed the Rumor Mill

The same goes for rumors about people changing companies. Let's say somebody comes to you with, "Tiffany said she might be joining another company," or "Sarah said she might be looking into another business opportunity." We can't allow ourselves to talk about these kinds of situations. Don't get into it by responding, "Are you serious? She really said that?" We have to stay very neutral and grounded. Whatever we hear, we do not repeat that to anyone else, unless it's something the person said publicly.

The only time we should quote someone is when the person made the communication from the stage. Even if we share a story as a learning experience, we should never have a name in our mouth. I see new leaders do this all the time. They don't mean to, but they get deeply into rumors or politics within their company, and it can make for very awkward situations.

Step Out of Your Comfort Zone—but Not Too Far!

Growing into business leadership will require you to step out of your comfort zone. Here is my recommendation: don't take a huge leap. When you're coming out of your comfort zone, don't try to go five miles. Instead, start with one step. By taking baby steps, trust you're going to get there.

For instance, I have lots of girls on my team who are scared of presenting or training in front of groups. When someone's ready to take that first step, I say, "I'd like to have you share your story on my conference call next week." That pushes them one step out of their comfort zone. Then the next time I'll say, "I'm going to have you on a webinar where attendees can actually see you." That pushes them a little bit more. The next step is, "We're going to do a training in your area, I'd like for you to be on a panel." That pushes them a little more. Then the ultimate step for them is to be a presenter at a live event. Taking it one step at a time is not as scary and allows you to grow along the way.

I actually have a girl who wouldn't even do videos. Now she's going to be a speaker at one of our company events. When she heard the news, she said, "How did you get me to do this, Amber? I didn't agree to this." I said, "You're going to love it," and I know she will. She grew into that position one step at a time.

Follow the System, but Find Your Style

As leaders we want to foster duplication in our businesses. However, we also want people to keep or develop their personal style. For instance, if I started to speak or act like a salesperson, I'd probably look really dumb, because it's not my personality. People would sense that I was uncomfortable and not being myself. We all have to find a way to build our business that suits our personal style. We want to be authentic and feel good about what we are doing.

When I was just starting to build my brand, I asked a friend in the network marketing profession, "Should I make videos with network marketing tips like you do?" This was when I had not trained very many people yet.

She gave me some good advice. She said, "You felt a little uncomfortable at our last leadership retreat, so maybe not yet. You are awesome at giving product demonstrations. Start doing videos on the product and build up your self-confidence. Develop more of a following, and then once you have trained a few more leaders yourself, you can do training videos with business tips. That way you're going to be more comfortable in front of the camera, too."

It's always about being comfortable and authentic. We never should try to fake it. If you see your business sponsor doing something that's totally not you, don't try to make it you, because it's going to come off as very unnatural.

➤ Don't Buy Excuses, Including Your Own

To learn how to handle other people's excuses, we first have to look at our own. I had to step outside myself (as if I were somebody else looking in) to realize I had more excuses than I thought. When my business was not growing, I told myself, "My husband works. I'm with the kids. I don't have that much time to build my business." That was an excuse, a wall I built up in my mind that kept me separate from my goal.

Excuses can be anything. A common one is, "I don't have enough money to get started," or "I don't know enough people." These are all excuses, and if you believe in them, you're not going to succeed. There is no excuse for not succeeding; you can get around any obstacle if you really want to. I've figured that out by now. A lot of us carry around excuses—and we don't even realize it.

Up until recently, I was carrying around a few extra pounds I gained in the last two years, because we actually had money to spend on delicious family and business dinners. I had a whole litany of excuses for my lack of fitness. "I homeschool. I'm building a business. I'm traveling all the time. I don't have time to work out." I needed to give myself my own advice, my own coaching: *excuses exist only in our minds.*

Ever since I caught myself making excuses for my extra weight, I've been doing squats while I'm making lunch, walking the kids to the park the long way, and working out a little while I'm there. I realized I was just standing in my own way, so I broke my own barrier. There's an excuse for everything, and we sometimes lean on it as a crutch. To help others realize this and overcome their excuses, I share my personal story of how we all have them and how I find my way around them.

➤ Use Momentum and Create Breakthroughs

Some people think they need to know everything before they can start growing their business. "I'm going to go through the starter kit." "I'm going to take two months and study the comp plan." "I first want to know every detail about the products." If it's a weight loss product, maybe I want to take it for a while myself and get my before-and-after photos before I actually start building the business. People who start slow often don't stay excited, because they aren't seeing a check.

My goal is get new people earning a check from their business as soon as possible. We want to build on their excitement and create momentum. The faster you start, the easier it is to keep going and growing. Momentum means that once an object is in motion, it tends to stay in motion. It's like with my kids riding their bicycle up the hill. They go up a little, and they roll down. It may take a while to get up that hill, but once the wheels start rolling, they keep rolling, and you go faster and faster. That's how momentum works.

Once you start using momentum, your business will be on a growth curve. In the meantime, you will notice that your success in network marketing is not linear. You may be doing the right actions and progressing with your mindset, and your business is building kind of slowly, and then all of a sudden there is this exponential growth or quantum leap. It's like planting seeds—everything is growing underground, so we don't always see it.

The Harvest Cannot Be Prevented

I tell my team, "Just keep planting your seeds—and know it may be many days until you can harvest them." What you do today may not seem like it's doing much. You may be talking to five people a day, building those relation-ships, and two weeks go by and still nothing happens. So people think, "I should just quit." I've seen this happen so many times. The truth is, they simply didn't give it enough time to mature. They didn't stay around long enough to get to the harvest.

If you work your business patiently and consistently, you will eventually experience a breakthrough that catapults you to an entirely new level of success. This is how a network marketing business works. Expect success and know that planting and harvesting does not happen in the same season. What you plant and nourish *must* bring forth its fruit. It's a natural law: *the harvest cannot be prevented.* If you stick with it, you will meet with success.

Chapter 10
Summary

1. How to Handle Drama and Gossip

2. Don't Feed the Rumor Mill

3. Step Out of Your Comfort Zone—but Not Too Far!

4. Follow the System, but Find Your Style

5. Don't Buy Excuses, Including Your Own

6. Use Momentum and Expect Breakthroughs

7. The Harvest Cannot Be Prevented

11

The Power of Events

*"This is the power of gathering:
it inspires us, delightfully, to be
more hopeful, more joyful, more
thoughtful: in a word, more alive."*

—Alice Waters

At my first company event, I remember thinking, "These people are crazy." At that time, I didn't have any success. Dave told me, "Everybody who's doing this, they're not broke! Would you rather look cool and be broke, or would you rather have fun, maybe feel a little silly at first, and have money in our bank account?" I said, "Being broke is not cool. I want to do this." I had built up a wall. I was too cool for it, until I realized having your utilities shut off wasn't cool either.

DAVE The very first event we went to, we pretty much skipped our house payment so we could get there. Our upline had told us, "You have to be there if you want success," so we made it work.

When we got there and walked in, we could feel the energy of the place—music blasting, everybody's happy, people high-fiving each other. We sat down, the event starts, and the first trainer takes us through some exercises.

I stand up and start doing them, because in my mind that's what you're supposed to do. I look behind me, and Amber's sitting down in her chair, arms crossed, staring down at the ground. She eventually looks up at me, shaking her head, as in, "I am not doing this stuff. This is ridiculous."

I felt foolish being up there by myself while she was sitting down. I nudged her and said, "Get up here! We came here so you could be part of this." It's just kind of funny to see where she came from—and the contrast of where she is today.

Just recently at Eric Worre's *Go Pro Recruiting Mastery* event in Las Vegas, people were lining up for two hours simply to take a picture and say hi to Amber. It's funny how far your mindset can take you when you change your thinking and actually let your defenses down a little bit.

➤ Open Your Mind to a New Culture

When I opened my mind and started participating in my company's events, everything began to change. I understand if you, like I did, feel a little resistance to this new environment. For most of us, it's a brand new culture we've never been part of. At our 9-to-5 jobs, we don't go around high-fiving each other or doing silly exercises. Then again, if we did, our job might be a much better place to work. All I had to do was open up my mind for some new possibilities. I'm sure you can do this, too.

Events are where you build the foundation of your business. It's not something the company puts on to make money. Typically they don't even make a profit; they're happy if they break even. Remember, events are where we recharge our batteries. Being surrounded by thousands of people who share the same mindset and goals similar to our own is a powerful experience. Attending events is absolutely critical for growing a network marketing business.

When people ask me, "What's your secret to success?" my answer is, *personal development* and *events*. Being around that energy makes a huge impact.

➤ Be Fully Present and Participate

There are a few things I see new people do at events that I warn against. The first one is using events as a time to see their friends in the business. They're out in the hallway talking while the training is going on inside. That is *not* what you need to be doing. You need to be in your seat, taking notes and paying attention. There's a time to get together with your team *after* the training. There's a time and a place for socializing. It drives me nuts when I see people hanging out at the bar or talking when they could be in the room learning.

Another one is people who don't really pay attention. They're present physically, but they're not there mentally—and that's not going to help them. They're not going to learn anything. They're going to go home and have the same results as they had before the event. It's very important to be fully present and focused. It took money, time, and effort to be at that event, so get the most out of it.

Once you get home, don't let everything you learned sit in your notebook. *Take action.* If you don't take action, what's the point? For your business to grow, you have to put what you learned into practice. Events are awesome, if you use them to your advantage. They are also exhausting, and so much fun. Being at events is what changed my mindset—and it will change yours, too!

➤ Events Provide Community and Social Proof

Here's how I convey the importance of attending events to new people. I say, "Everybody who is making money in the company is going to be there, and that's not a coincidence. *If you want what they have, you need to do what they do.*" I have girls who ate peanut butter and jelly sandwiches for the entire event weekend, because that's all they could afford after buying their ticket and paying for the hotel. I remember Dave and I living on protein shakes for weeks so we could afford to go to our company convention.

Sure, you can attend events online—we have lots of virtual parties and trainings—but it's nothing like getting together face to face, where you can actually meet people, hug somebody, and see their face when you're talking. Live events are powerful. Having people in the room who have had success provides social proof. When I organize opportunity meetings, we include lots of testimonials—for the business and for the product. When people see others who are where they want to be, it boosts their belief in a big way.

Events also create that feeling of belonging. A lot of people join network marketing not just for the money, but also for the community it provides. Attending those live events fills that need to belong like nothing else can. This is just as true for company events as it is for generic training events. I started attending generic events early on in my network marketing career. It made me grow a deep love and respect for the network marketing community and profession beyond my own company.

Generic Events Build Belief in the Profession

No matter what company we are in, we all have the same goal of wanting to change our lives and other people's lives. My first generic training event was Eric Worre's *Go Pro Recruiting Mastery* event. I absolutely loved meeting people from other companies, because we had so much in common, and there was a mutual understanding. I met some of my closest friends at these events, and we've helped each other out on several occasions.

I love the masterminding that takes place. Maybe these leaders from other companies are doing something I can adapt into my business and vice versa. When you bring a goal and intent to the event, big things can happen. Hearing from top earners in different companies is incredibly enriching. That's why I encourage all my team members to attend generic events as often as they can.

Some leaders don't like to send their new people to generic training events for fear that they might get confused, distracted, or overwhelmed. I don't have this concern at all. I *want* my girls to go. Anything they can get their hands on that is going to help their business, I want them to do.

For instance, I regularly participate in webinars or events for the Association of Network Marketing Professionals. I recently did a Google hangout with bestselling author Michelle Gielan to help launch her new book *Broadcasting Happiness* into the network marketing space. I don't directly profit from this effort. I just love to give my support, and I believe that by helping others with their goals, more good things are going to come to me.

➤ Respect No-Recruiting Zones!

One caveat: when you go to these events, don't recruit people for your business. Don't go there thinking you'll be able to increase your check by getting new clients or new business partners. That's not what these events are for, and if you do approach people with that mindset, nobody's going to want to talk to you. Nobody's going to want to follow you, because the leaders who are there love their businesses and companies.

On the other hand, I've received some amazing referrals from making friends with people in other companies. If they know someone who's interested in my company, they might say to them, "I have this amazing person who's my friend. She's never tried to recruit me. She's such a great person. Let me connect you with her." I've gotten a few of my top leaders this way without even trying . . . just by building connections. Once people like and trust you, and they know somebody who is looking for your business opportunity or product, they're going to refer you.

These events also attract some people who are looking for a change, people who aren't 100 percent happy with where they are. Naturally connecting with them and sharing your story may inspire them and make them want to follow you. My whole philosophy in network marketing, and it's served me well, is simply to care about people regardless of whether they will help me grow my check.

➤ Handy Tip: Make Generic Networking Cards

To make sure you don't come across as trying to recruit people into your business, you can create generic networking cards instead of passing out regular business cards with your company logo. I made some that simply show my title, Dream Creator, and my personal information. Now you feel totally free to hand your card out, and you'll never be labeled as "that person who was trying to recruit."

DAVE As a support partner, you need to understand that going to events is part of building the business. You may get irritated when you think your spouse is spending too much time away from the family or is just going out to have a good time. Know that the purpose of events is to learn how to build the business more efficiently, and in the long run, everyone benefits.

If, as a husband, you feel a little jealous of your wife's business taking too much of her time, know that it will not always be this way. Just keep supporting her, because the payoff is worth it. Would you rather have your wife leave for an event a few times per year, or have her spend 40 hours a week away from home at a job?

Ever since I retired from my job in 2013, I attend all events with Amber because we want to learn and grow together. Sometimes when people are lining up to get a picture with her, it can get a bit overwhelming. Seeing her in this environment feels weird because she is my wife and the mom of our kids.

While she's just another person, I see that Amber is changing a lot of people's lives, so they have a really strong emotional attachment to her. I try not to get in the way of that, because it's important for people to connect with her. It's helping them grow as leaders and even as people in general. I try to support that the best way I can.

When husbands see their wives grow into leadership positions, they're going to be proud. The attention you get at events with people following you everywhere can get a little overwhelming, especially when you're trying to use the restroom or get back to your room, and you're stopped every single step of the way. Instead of getting frustrated, I try to think of the lives I'm changing. I tell myself, "It's just a weekend."

I also remind myself of what happened to me a long time ago. I was at a company event and asked my upline, a top earner in the company, if I could take a picture with him. He was so nice and friendly on stage I was sure he wouldn't mind. When I approached him, he was by himself, and he refused to stop and let me take his picture. I remember feeling so small; I promised myself I would never make anyone feel that way. Now, every time I get a little frustrated or impatient when people want my time or attention, this story helps me to keep going—even when I'm tired. There is no greater joy for me than to go to sleep knowing I've brightened someone's day or inspired them to continue pursuing their dreams.

Chapter 11
Summary

1. Open Your Mind to a New Culture

2. Be Fully Present and Participate

3. Events Provide Community and Social Proof

4. Generic Events Build Belief in the Profession

5. Respect No-Recruiting Zones!

6. Handy Tip: Make Generic Networking Cards

12

Belief, Gratitude, and Faith

> "Unless you become like little children, you will never enter the kingdom of heaven."
>
> —Matthew 18:3

One of the biggest things you can do for your team members is to believe in them. Most people who start a network marketing business have never done anything like this before. Sometimes we forget that. When you have been in the network marketing profession for a while, it changes our perspective. As we spend more and more time hanging out with seasoned networkers, we can lose touch with how it feels to be brand new to all of this.

New people generally don't have that much belief in themselves, because they've never owned or built a business. As leaders, we need to believe in them, even before they believe in themselves. I mentored a friend of mine when she was just starting out, and now she is at the top of her company. She absolutely did it herself and I will never take credit for her success, but she told me, "The reason I was able to do it is because you believed in me. I was a girl living in a house with cockroaches. I didn't think I could be at the top of a company." At 21 years old, she did it, because I knew she would. From day one, I told her, "I already know what your future's going to look like. We just need to line the universe up with it."

Believe in People Before They Believe in Themselves

Believing in people can make a huge difference in how they feel and perform. So often, nobody believes in us. You go to work, you don't get a pat on the back. You're expected to do your job, and nobody gives you any credit. Recognition and belief go hand in hand. When you recognize people, look for the smallest accomplishments. It can be someone's first sale, even if it's not a very big one. They sell one product? Love on them. Shout it out on Facebook. Send them a message. Call them on

the phone and say, "Great job!" It will boost their confidence, and they're going to want to do more because
it feels good to be recognized. It also helps them build
belief in themselves, in the company, and in the network
marketing profession.

Believe in Yourself, Your Company, and the Business Model

Yes, believe in network marketing and believe success will
happen for you. Many people get in and after six months
they are disappointed and say, "I'm still not making six
figures." They don't believe in the process. It's like when
you go to school to be a doctor for eight years; the first six
months of your internship you're not going to do open-
heart surgery on anybody. You have to grow into that position and trust the process. People try to rush it and think,
"I didn't make a ton of money. This isn't for me." They
quit before they're ready to shine. If I had quit four years
ago, I wouldn't be where I am today. Quitting too soon is
so common, and it's due to people's lack of belief in the
process and in themselves.

Be Patient and Trust the Process

I climbed up very quickly in my current company, but
that's only because of all the work I had done before. I've
had a network marketing business since 2004, and everyone told me to quit. No one believed in me other than my
husband. We just kept going. We didn't listen to everybody
else. We let it go in one ear and out the other, because
we had this belief that it could happen. You don't know

when, but it's going to happen—as long as you don't quit. A lot of people get impatient. If they had just kept going—believing in themselves, investing in their personal development, and fine-tuning their people skills—they would have created a life they could only imagine.

"In this business you can't fail, as long as you don't quit."

—*Jimmy Smith*

What will make your journey to success a lot easier and more joyful is being grateful for what you already have. When you're thankful for something, you're going to get more. It's kind of like Christmastime. When you give your kids a present and they don't like it and aren't grateful, you don't want to give them anything else. But when they receive a present and they're happy and grateful, you want to keep blessing them with more. You want to keep giving, because you love feeling their joy and appreciation. You love the energy they're sending out. The universe works the same way.

➤ Be Grateful and Appreciate What You Have

I always tell my team, if you're thankful for what you have right now, the universe will reward you with more. When we were living in our mobile home, there were holes in the wall and the floor, yet I was grateful. I was thankful our family had a roof over our head, even though it leaked. We were happy we weren't homeless. We tried to make it better. We painted the walls, put rugs down, and bought a new stove. Dave's parents bought us a new washer and dryer. We were grateful as we made improvements. That's why we only stayed there for a short while. After eight months, we moved into a beautiful home, a single-family house and the best place we ever lived. It was all because we were grateful.

Even if you don't have much, you can appreciate what you have. Be grateful for your current position in your company; otherwise, you're not going to rank advance. Acknowledge yourself and be happy for what you've already accomplished.

DAVE When I was young, my mom taught me that you can't get more of what you want if you're not grateful for and taking care of what you already have. She said, "God will give you only what you can handle, so first show Him you can handle what you already have, so He can bless you with more." If you live in gratitude, the outcome will be an abundant life. You also need to have faith. Gratitude and faith go hand in hand.

➤ Can a Christian Believe in the Law of Attraction?

Speaking of faith, a lot of people on my team ask me, "You say you're a Christian, and you believe in God. Then you talk about the universe and the Law of Attraction. How do these go together?" For me, there is no contradiction. Everybody has their own beliefs. No matter what higher power you believe in, that is what created the universe for you. For me, God created the universe. He also created the Law of Attraction.

If you are a Buddhist, you may be using another name for what you consider to be the Source of all things. While I don't know much about other religions, I do believe there's a higher power, no matter what you might call it, and I believe this higher power created the Law of Attraction and the universe for each of us to use and create our own best life.

People ask, "If you believe in God, why do you thank the universe?" I said, "Ultimately, I'm thanking God, because He created the universe." The universe is so vast and we are so complex, our brains cannot possibly comprehend it. That's why we have to let down our walls, those barriers that don't let us see beyond what's logical. The fact that we think thoughts, attach a feeling to them, and then they happen—that's not logical! It's not something we can easily wrap our minds around.

› Childlike Faith Will Help You Create Your Dream

Sometimes the hardest part is unlearning what you've been taught and looking beyond that part of your brain that needs to understand everything. Be like a kid again. Kids don't think, "How is it possible that Santa Claus can come to every single house in one night?" They believe in their dream and have faith. Once you lower those walls and believe beyond a shadow of a doubt that success is going to happen, things will start happening for you. How did somebody figure out how to build a skyscraper? They had to think about it first. Everything you see in this world started out with a thought in someone's mind.

DAVE Think back to when you were a kid and how openly you looked at anything you saw for the very first time. You didn't push it away because you didn't understand it. I call it a child's mind or child-like faith. When you're a child, you can have faith in anything. You can believe you'll be an astronaut—and it motivates you to study. As we get older, we kind of get beaten down by the system and into thinking that's not the right way to be anymore. We become our own dream stealers. Losing our dreams typically happens when we become adults. We should never lose our capacity to dream.

When I was living in that mobile home, I didn't think that was my ending. I knew it was just temporary. I had faith in myself and knew I could have the life I desired. You want to see it in your mind first before it can actually become reality. You have to believe in it. If your faith is limited or shaky, it will be much harder to create your new reality. You really have to know it to be true before it actually happens.

"*You will see it when you believe it, and not a minute sooner!*"

—*Jimmy Smith*

Once you have the right mindset, success is a foregone conclusion. The secret to having it all is believing you already do. When you truly know your *why,* the universe opens up and graciously provides you with everything you need to succeed. Now it's your turn to go out, put into practice what you've learned, and have faith. I've shared what I know, and I'm cheering you on. I believe in you!

Chapter 12
Summary

1. Believe in People Before They Believe in Themselves

2. Believe in Yourself, Your Company, and the Business Model

3. Be Patient and Trust the Process

4. Be Grateful and Appreciate What You Have

5. Can a Christian Believe in the Law of Attraction?

6. Childlike Faith Will Help You Create Your Dream

Acknowledgments

I want to thank all the people who have guided me on my path and helped me write this book through their example and inspiration. I'm especially grateful for . . .

My husband for always supporting me.

My three beautiful boys, Brice, Brayden, and Carter, for being my biggest cheerleaders!

My team—*you are amazing!*

Eric Worre, who has taught me so much.

Dr. Josephine Gross, who took our conversations and somehow turned them into this book. Her listening and writing skills made the process easy and fun. I love how she captured my voice.

Chris Gross, for always giving me professional advice.

Reed Bilbray and Sandra Bienkowski, who helped bring this book to life.

Doug Firebaugh, for believing in me when I first got started.

Jordan Adler, Lisa Grossmann, Garrett and Sylvia McGrath, Josh Wyles, Tim and Jill Herr, Cindy and Joshua Denne, and John and Tiffany Malott, for their continuing friendship and support.

Recommended Resource List

➤ Books

Beach Money by Jordan Adler

The Four-Year Career by Richard Bliss Brooke

How to Win Friends and Influence People by Dale Carnegie

Building an Empire by Brian Carruthers

The Flip-Flop CEO by Janine Finney and Lory Muirhead

Think and Grow Rich by Napoleon Hill

The Slight Edge by Jeff Olson

Rock Your Network Marketing Business by Sarah Robbins

Be, Do, and Have More by Presley Swagerty

Go Pro: 7 Steps to Becoming a Network Marketing Professional by Eric Worre

Videos

The Abundance Factor documentary by Riley Dayne

Rise of the Entrepreneur documentary by Eric Worre

Audios

What Would You Change if Your Annual Income Suddenly Became Your Monthly Income audio by Bob Proctor

Building Your Network Marketing Business audio by Jim Rohn

The Lotus Code audio and workbook by Mark Yarnell and Valerie Bates

About the Author

mber Voight is the mother of three young boys, a wife, a friend, and a multiple six-figure earner in network marketing. From her home in Minnesota, she leads a growing international team of close to 100,000 members spread out over North America, Australia, and the United Kingdom. Amber reached the highest rank in her company in just three months using her business savvy, social media networking skills, and passion for helping others.

Amber hasn't always been successful in her network marketing business. For many years, she failed, and failed, and failed! She was always looking for "the next big opportunity" without working on herself, going from company to company, wondering why it just wasn't working for her, wishing she could somehow become like the leaders she saw on stage at her company conventions . . .

Then one day it clicked! Amber realized she had to work on her mindset and attitude so she could become the leader others would want to follow. She immersed herself in personal development and learned all she could about the network marketing profession. Today, Amber's passion is to share the strategies and methods she used to become a top earner and leader in her company.

Amber wrote *The 7-Cent Decision* so anyone can learn from her mistakes and build on what brought her success. Amber always keeps it real and tells you exactly how she did it. Now that she has reached some major milestones in her career and built a dream life for her family, she loves to give others the tools, belief, and support they need to achieve their goals and dreams.

Buy Multiple Copies
of *The 7-Cent-Decision*
TO SHARE WITH YOUR
PROSPECTS AND TEAM!

Help prospects and team members build belief in themselves and network marketing while giving them a blueprint and proven methods for success.

For bulk purchases and quantity pricing,
please call 866 343 4005/int'l 818 727 2000

Or email info@7centdecision.com

HIRE *Amber*

TO SPEAK OR TRAIN AT YOUR EVENT

Let Amber inspire and teach your team members how to

➤ Set goals, overcome limiting belies, and create results.

➤ Develop business and leadership skills to grow and rank advance.

➤ Build a solid team of self-motivated, committed entrepreneurs.

➤ Use social media effectively for increasing business and building culture.

➤ Create a balanced life of fun, financial peace, fulfillment, and contribution.

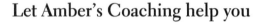

Connect with Amber

➤ Be inspired by uplifting posts,
tips, and stories.

➤ Join a growing community of
like-minded entrepreneurs.

➤ Let Amber help you stay motivated to work
and grow your business.

➤ See how she uses social media to stand out
from the crowd and attract followers.

➤ Have fun with connecting and sharing while
growing yourself and your income.

facebook.com/
networkingwithamber

YouTube.com/
themlmqueen

@ambervoight

amber_voight

@ambervoight

@ambervoight

WWW.AMBERVOIGHT.COM

WWW.7CENTDECISION.COM